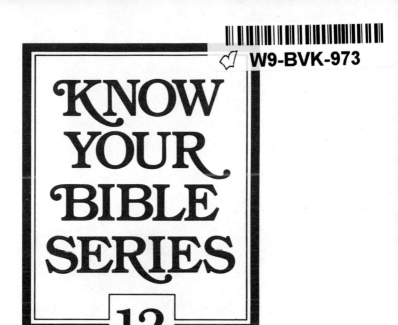

KNOW YOUR BIBLE SERIES

12

MATTHEW
MARK
LUKE
ACTS

ROY L. SMITH

ABINGDON PRESS
NASHVILLE

Matthew, Mark, Luke, Acts

No. 209234

Printed in U.S.A.

INTRODUCTION

Christianity originated in a great spiritual experience. A child was born in one of the outlying provinces of the Roman Empire who, when he had come to manhood, became a wandering teacher of religion. Because his ideas differed radically from those of his time and his people, he soon found himself involved in disputes with the authorities, and in the end paid for his convictions with his life. Following his death certain events occurred which convinced his followers that he was not dead, but that he continued alive and that he communicated with them by spiritual means.

The great central event which resulted in this conviction was his resurrection. Three days after his crucifixion he was seen alive, according to the solemn declaration of his friends, and in the course of the next few weeks several hundred people testified to the fact that they had heard him speak and had seen him in person. The affair created a sensation, and within the space of a very short time men in far places were to be heard telling the story and declaring their faith in him as the Son of God.

Very naturally such a man could not be ignored. Things he had said and done, which might otherwise have been forgotten or ignored, now took on new significance. His followers, first attracted by his compelling personality and by the things he had said, now began asking deep and difficult questions concerning him. Who was he? What was he? By what power did he live and teach? What was it that gave his words such authority? By what power did he rise above the ordinary facts of life and death?

A second fact was equally impressive: plain and humble people began declaring, with the utmost solemnity and sincerity, that the Risen One have communicated with them and guided them in spiritual matters. Mysteries were made plain, new truths were apprehended, spiritual tensions were dissolved, and life was redeemed. As a result, a new sense of peace and serenity pervaded their lives. They were transformed in mind and heart, so that they were made over and had become new creatures.

Because people were having such experiences, an effort was made to explain them. The first preachers of the Christian message were not theologians; they only told their experiences,

3

and testified to amazing things that had happened inside their own lives and the lives of their fellows. Their gospel was a faith, a report of a great personal experience, and not an orderly philosophy of religion.

As the years multiplied, however, problems arose within the Christian movement, which called for solutions, and great leaders offered advice, counsel, and argument. Great events "whose source was God and whose center was Jesus Christ" called for explanations. Coming in competition with the philosophies of the Greek world, the new religion was compelled to justify itself by logic and reason.

As the result of these and other conditions, Christian writings began to appear. Honest and earnest men put down on paper their most profound convictions, and this literature began to circulate throughout the world, both inside and outside Christian circles. No author, with the single exception of the author of Revelation, seems to have had any thought that his writing would ever be received as scripture, but when the Church had had time to study them all with care and test them in the crucible of experience, it was decided that certain of them were the product of the impress of the Spirit of God upon the minds of the writers. These were finally gathered together in the New Testament.

The three Gospels and the history which are surveyed in this study constitute the rock base of the Christian faith. In them are to be found all the basic facts we have concerning the life, teachings, and activities of Jesus of Nazareth. Protestantism has placed the Scriptures at the very center of its faith and rested its whole case upon their testimony, together with the validation of the Scriptures which has been provided by personal experience.

Roy L. Smith

4

Three Gospels
and a History

1 What does "gospel" mean?

The Greek word which has been translated "gospel" in our English New Testament meant "good news" to the ancients. Josephus, the famous Jewish historian, used it in that sense on numerous occasions. In broad terms, to the first-century Church, it meant to good news of salvation proclaimed by the Christians. In those days the word was used only in the singular, somewhat as we use the word "salvation." No one thought of applying it to a book, for the "good news" was not read but *preached*. Paul used it in that sense (Romans 1:16) and referred to the message of salvation which he preached as "my gospel" (Romans 2:16). Just as a modern writer would not think of using the plural form of "independence" or "justice," so the earliest Christians never spoke of the "Gospels."

2 How did the word "Gospels" come into use?

We have already learned, in the case of other books of the Bible, that the names by which we now know them were no part of the original writing. This was true also of the Gospels. For a considerable time the books which we now know as "the four Gospels" circulated independently without specific names. Each reported the Christian message, though from a different angle, and in time it became necessary to distinguish between them. Had there been but one such book, it would probably have been called simply "The Gospel"; but, because there were at least four, they were given descriptive names, and in that fact we find a very important clue.

3 What clue is furnished by the names?

In answering this question two facts must be kept in mind: (1) A Greek preposition is used in the title of each Gospel which is translated "according to" in our English New Testament. That translation, however, does not convey the full meaning of the word. The original Greek word implies that there were several Gospels and that the Gospel *According to* Matthew is only one of them. (2) The title does not say that the individual named is the author of all the statements made in the writing, but that he is believed to be the one responsible for sending it out as a statement of the Christian message of good news.

4 What is the significance of all that?

When we say a book is "by" a certain writer, we mean that all the statements it contains originated with that writer. And parts of which he is not the actual author are indicated by quotation marks. But the ancient authors used no punctuation marks of any kind, and when they quoted from another writer they had to state the fact if they desired to give him credit. It often happened that they quoted without such identification. In such cases no one held the author under any obligation to credit the source from which he took the quotation. In the case of the four Gospels of the New Testament it was understood by those who read them first that the material had been gleaned from a variety of sources and that, while some of it might be derived from personal knowledge, other parts had been taken from other sources. That the writers gleaned with a purpose, and that they presented their material with a definite viewpoint in mind, was well understood. Christians of the first century regarded them as different "versions" of the essential "gospel" with which all were familiar. Therefore the titles of the four books actually meant "the good news of salvation through Jesus Christ as told by" Matthew, Mark, Luke, or John.

5 When were the titles given to the books?

The original writings were put out without any titles of any kind; but as other versions appeared some identification was needed, and they were given names. When this occurred we do not know. We do know, however, that the earliest form of the title in the case of Mark's Gospel varied considerably, for there are differences in the oldest Greek manuscripts now in our possession. In one such the title consists of only two words which, being translated, mean "According to Mark." The word "Gospel" was added sometime later—about the middle of the second century, in the opinion of many scholars. The fact that it did not appear in the earliest manuscripts raises a very important subject.

What is the significance of the absence
6 of the word "Gospel"?

There was no official statement of the basic facts of the Christian message for many years following the death of Jesus. There was, however, a considerable body of information concerning the Master and his teachings which passed among the Christians in the form of teachings, sayings, anecdotes, etc. To all this the scholars have given the name "oral tradition," and some understanding of this is essential to any thorough understanding of the New Testament. In its broadest sense the first "gospel" preached by the Christians rested back on this oral tradition.

In the case of the first three Gospels each writer made large use of this "oral tradition," putting down what was, in his opinion, the core of the Christian belief. Each, of course, presented it from his own personal angle to serve his own purpose; but all were dependent, in the last analysis, upon the same general source materials. The absence of the word "Gospel" from the early title of Mark's book suggests that the first readers did not accept it as a complete statement of the Christian message, but only as a statement "according to Mark."

7 What is the meaning of "oral tradition"?

An amazing person named Jesus of Nazareth had appeared in Palestine. He went about teaching the people with unusual power and authority (Mark 1:22), quite unlike that of any other man of his time. So remarkable were the things he said and did that he attracted wide attention and set men wondering. Then came the stupendous climax of his career when, having been crucified, he was seen alive on numerous occasions afterward by a considerable number of people. Much talk concerning him went through Palestine (Acts 10:37), many stories were told of his activities, and many of his sayings were repeated over and over. The climactic fact of his resurrection convinced men that he was somehow divine, and furnished the reason for their devotion to him after his death. It aroused vast interest in everything concerning him, and the large number of stories about him and the principles he taught, which circulated among the people, became what the scholars call "the oral tradition."

8 Was it written down?

So far as our New Testament record shows, Jesus himself did no writing. The only occasion when any mention is made of his writing is that related in John 8:1-11, when he scrawled a few words in the dust at his feet. None of the Gospels make any claim to having been written by eyewitnesses, though one does say that considerable writing had been done (Luke 1:1), some part of which may have been by persons who had seen and heard Jesus in person. The Christian Church came into existence at a time, however, when the masses were reached by the spoken word in most matters, and by the written word to only a very limited degree. Jesus was a man of the people who went about among them preaching and teaching, and the Christian tradition followed the customs of the times. Just as many modern fraternal orders hand down their rituals, vows, and "secrets" by word of mouth, so the ancient Christians preserved their traditions and teachings very largely by the oral method.

9 Were no eyewitness records made?

It is impossible to make positive statements in this matter, for no precise evidence exists to prove or disprove them. There are those who argue, with some reason, that Matthew—sometimes called Levi (Mark 2:14)—made some notes of the Master's sayings and that these circulated in written form at an early date. This might be true, for Matthew was a Roman official of considerable importance and must have been trained by the requirements of his profession as a tax collector to make written records. Luke's introduction to his Gospel (1:1-2) strongly suggests that eyewitness accounts were in existence at the time he wrote, but such records as there were could have been no more than fragmentary for a good many years after Jesus' death, for a very good reason.

10 Why should there have been no contemporary records?

Jesus' death seems to have taken his disciples by surprise. They had not anticipated such a tragic end but had expected that he would inaugurate a movement which would restore the Jews to their ancient power (Luke 24:21). He seems therefore to have died before anyone thought about writing his life. This is in no way surprising, for the full meaning of his amazing career did not appear until after his resurrection. It was this great fact which sent the world back to study his personality.

11 How reliable is the oral tradition?

To answer this question, it is necessary to describe the oral tradition a little more fully. Following Jesus' death four great centers developed from which Christian influences radiated—Jerusalem, Rome, Ephesus, and Antioch. The problems to be faced by the Christians might vary somewhat from center to center. In Jerusalem, for instance, the conspicuous problem might be that of conformity to the ancient Jewish Law, while in Antioch or Ephesus it might be the question of personal morals. Everywhere, however, men were asking, "What did Jesus teach?"

As a guide in solving problems of conduct and belief, sayings and teachings of Jesus were cited. Sometimes the answer might be found in a parable the Master had told, or in other cases a few sentences from one of his sermons might provide the answer. Gradually a body of tradition developed, based upon the Master's own life and teachings, composed probably of brief proverbs, stories, sayings, and parables. That this constituted a trustworthy account of Jesus' "gospel" may be believed for three reasons:

1. Eleven of his intimate friends—followers who were called "disciples"—survived him for many years and gave their lives to the task of perpetuating his memory and his teachings. As long as they lived, they were in a position to correct any errors.

2. Every saying, story, and report had to undergo the scrutiny of the entire Christian movement, and among the early followers of Jesus there were a very great many who were in a position to detect and identify mistakes or misunderstandings.

3. Practically all we know about those centuries and the men who were active in them has come down to us by the same process. All history, beliefs, customs, and knowledge were conserved and transmitted by the same methods used in the case of the New Testament. To indict it is to indict everything we know out of those times.

The core of the oral tradition, however, seems to have been the account of the resurrection. The story of Jesus' triumph over the grave seems to have been told wherever the Christians went preaching. Though it might vary here and there in details, the great basic facts were always the same.

12 Is the resurrection so important then?

It is the great, towering, unprecedented event about which the entire Christian movement grew up. Paul called the gospel "the word of the cross," and added that if the resurrection were not a fact, then the entire Christian position would collapse (I Corinthians 15:14), thus making the cross and the resurrection the twin bases of the movement. Even when all the values in Jesus' life and teachings have been conceded, it can still be said that if he had not risen from the dead, his beautiful life and career would have been forgotten and there would have been no Christian movement. His triumph over the grave authenticated the things he said and did, and created an interest in him which finally produced the Christian Church and the New Testament. There was, however, an additional reason why no contemporary biography of Jesus appeared.

13 What was the additional reason?

During the first few weeks or months following the ascension, Jesus' disciples were in a state of great confusion. At first they waited at Jerusalem as they had been commanded (Luke 24:49; Acts 1:4), and then, when the astounding experience of Pentecost fell upon them, they moved out into the world to preach their gospel. No small part of their message was a declaration that the Master would return shortly to set up his Kingdom, for it was admitted that he had not performed all the task assigned to the Messiah on the occasion of his first appearance. This expectation of an early return was so vivid that it discouraged the preparation of any written "life." Why should anyone go to the trouble of writing the record if Christ might be expected momentarily to put in a second appearance? The great fact which occupied the mind of the primitive Church was not his life but his resurrection. Paul's letters are excellent evidence at this point.

14 What do Paul's letters prove?

Even a casual reader of Paul's correspondence must have

been impressed by the fact that the Apostle makes very few references to historical events in Jesus' life, beyond the crucifixion and resurrection. One event (I Corinthians 11:23-25) and two sayings (Acts 20:35; I Corinthians 7:10-11) make up the list. It is very interesting to note that Paul makes no reference whatever to any story of the virgin birth, and bases no doctrine or argument thereon. His primary interest is in the cross and the resurrection.

15 What produced the Gospels then?

As the years went on and the Church grew, many affiliated themselves with the Christian movement who knew little or nothing about Jesus, his life, his teachings, or his character. It became necessary to provide such with authentic information. Then, too, those who had known him personally began to die and pass off the scene, and some dependable written record of his life and ministry became increasingly necessary. If Christianity was to take the world, men everywhere must be made familiar with the life and person of the one who inaugurated the movement. Just about this time, however, an entirely new factor entered the case. Persecutions began.

16 What effect did the persecutions have?

Reference has already been made, in connection with our study of the Fourth Gospel and Revelation, to the persecutions which broke out in the reigns of Nero and Domitian. In A.D. 64 the Emperor Nero accused the Christians of Rome of having fired the city, and ordered wholesale executions as a consequence. This had the effect of spreading consternation through the ranks of the Christians, and the Gospel of Mark bears distinct evidence of having been written for the purpose of exalting those who suffered for the cause. There is the suggestion of the bridegroom snatched away from his bride (2:20); James and John are warned of their martyrdom (10:39); there are numerous sentences which would have been read with peculiar understanding by those who had seen their fellow Christians tossed to the lions (8:34-38; 13:9-23). The Gospel of Mark seems to have been written for the distinct purpose of nerving the Christians to stand firm in their faith.

17   Which Gospel was written first?

By almost universal agreement among scholars of all shades of opinion, the honor of being the first of the four Gospels to come to its present form is ascribed to the Gospel of Mark.

18   When was Mark written?

Irenaeus, one of the earliest Church Fathers and a writer whose opinions have been found to be quite reliable, says that both Mark and Luke were written sometime after the deaths of Peter and Paul, and these are believed to have occurred during the Neronian persecutions in A.D. 64-65. We shall discover, when we come to a detailed study of Matthew and Luke, that the first and third Gospels lean heavily upon Mark. Inasmuch as we know that both were compiled before the end of the first century, there seems to be general agreement that Mark must have been written sometime between A.D. 65 and A.D. 70. The majority opinion seems to favor the latter date (about forty years after the death of Jesus). The student will, therefore, be on safe ground if he assumes that the Gospel appeared approximately in its present form about A.D. 70. The precise date cannot be fixed.

19   Who wrote the Gospel of Mark?

Here again we must look first inside the book itself for evidence. Doing so, we will discover that, so far as the text itself is concerned, it is anonymous. Without Mark's name attached to the title we would have no direct hint as to the author's identity. Our next step is to look outside the book for any evidence that may throw light on the question.

20   Is there any such evidence?

Clement of Alexandria, one of the great scholars of the Church, toward the close of the second century wrote that Mark prepared the book at the request of the congregation at Rome. Irenaeus, writing sometime between 174 and 189, says that "Mark, the disciple and interpreter of Peter, also transmitted to us in writing those things which Peter had preached." Eusebius, the first great historian of the Church after the author of the Acts, quotes a statement from Papias, bishop of

Hierapolis in Asia Minor, which must be dated about A.D. 140, and which is extremely interesting for two reasons.

21 What is Papias' statement?

First of all, the bishop made the statement that he preferred the living voice to the things which were written in books, and for that reason he made diligent inquiry of anyone who was able to tell him anything about the words and deeds of the Apostles. One from whom he had received much information and inspiration was "John the presbyter," whom he describes as "one of the disciples of the Lord." This, of course, meant a faithful follower of Christ, and not one of the original band of eleven. The further meaning of this statement is very interesting, for it was Papias' way of saying that he preferred the oral tradition to the record which was written in a book. This is evidence that Christian writings were not yet fully accepted. If there is any doubt in the student's mind concerning the reliability of the oral tradition, the word of the bishop of Hierapolis should be very reassuring. Those second-century Christians trusted it further than they did a written record, and, we must remember, they were living very close to the original events.

On the subject of the authorship of Mark, Papias quotes the "presbyter John" as having said: "Mark, having become the interpreter of Peter, wrote down accurately, though not indeed in order, whatsoever things he remembered of the things said or done by Christ. For he neither heard the Lord nor followed him, but afterwards, as I said, he followed Peter, who adapted his teachings to the needs [of the hearers], but with no intention of giving a connected account of the Lord's discourses. So that Mark committed no error in writing some things as he remembered them. For he was careful of one thing, not to omit any of the things which he had heard, and not to state any of them falsely."

22 Does this settle the matter?

There remain two additional facts to be considered. First, there is no contradictory evidence of any kind refuting the Marcan authorship, it being admitted that no other name has ever been attached to the book. If Mark was not the author-compiler, then we have not the slightest clue as to who that one may have been, for no other name has ever been suggested.

The second fact, which consists of a single reference (14:12), is extremely interesting. A dispute had arisen among the churches concerning the proper date for celebrating Easter. The churches of Asia—Ephesus, Smyrna, Colossae, etc.—observed Nisan 14, the Jewish date for the Passover. Because it was a fixed date, it might fall on any day of the week and only occasionally on Sunday. A considerable number of the western churches, led by the congregation at Rome, celebrated the great Christian festival on Sunday. A fragment of writing from a certain Apollinaris has come down to us setting forth the Roman position. It reads, "On the 14th the Lord ate the sheep with his disciples, but himself suffered on the great day of unleavened bread." This is an attempt to date the death of Jesus as subsequent to the Passover.

23 What does this mean?

It means that the Roman Church dated the crucifixion on "the great day of unleavened bread," and that Mark, in writing his book, fixed the date to conform to that position (14:12). Our interest in the verse, however, grows out of the light it throws on the question of Mark's authorship.

24 What light can it throw on the question of authorship?

From various references in the writings of the ancient Church Fathers we know that Mark was a resident of Rome. Then, also, in First Peter there appears a sentence, "She [the church] who is at Babylon [Rome] . . . sends you greetings; and so does my son Mark" (5:13), which locates Mark in the capital. The natural conclusion is that Mark wrote the Gospel for the church at Rome and in doing so assumed the Roman position on the subject of the Easter date.

25 Who was this man Mark?

The name "Marcus"—"Mark" is the English form—was Roman rather than Jewish and was in more or less common use at the time. There is, however, but one individual by that name

14

well identified in the New Testament. He was a somewhat inconspicuous member of the Christian community in Jerusalem, the son of a woman who owned a house sufficiently commodious to accommodate meetings of the church. (Acts 12:12). There are those who profess to believe that he was the young man referred to in Mark 14:51 and that he was afterward converted to the Christian faith by Peter (I Peter 5:13; I Corinthians 4:15). Barnabas was somehow related to the family (Colossians 4:10) and became responsible for introducing the young man to Paul (Acts 15:37). The great Apostle seems to have conceived a poor opinion of the young man after one rather disappointing experience (Acts 15:37-40), and broke with Barnabas on account of it. Later, as it appears from his letters, Paul revised this opinion somewhat (Colossians 4:10; Philemon 23-24; II Timothy 4:11), and held Mark in considerable esteem. By some means of which we have no knowledge the youth later became associated with Peter and the church at Rome, serving the Apostle in something of the capacity of a secretary-interpreter.

26 Why did Peter need an interpreter?

He was by birth a Galilean and was reared, as was Jesus also, to speak Aramaic, a language similar to Hebrew and commonly used in Palestine. Inasmuch as Greek was spoken among the Roman Christians, it was necessary for someone to interpret for Peter, and, according to the testimony of several early Church Fathers, this was Mark's responsibility.

27 How was he prepared for the task?

His Roman name suggests that the author was one of the Greek-speaking Jews, or Hellenists, of whom there were many in Jerusalem in Jesus' day. The fact that his Gospel treats the question of Sabbath observance lightly (2:23-28) and holds the ceremonial washings in some contempt (7:1-17) indicates that he shared in the Hellenistic liberalism. There are, however, three special facts concerning the author which should be noted with care.

28 What is the first fact?

He is evidently familiar with the Jewish scriptures (1:2; 2:25-28; 7:6; 7:10; 11:17; 12:26, 29-30, 36; 14:21, 27; 15:28). His quotations, however, are always from the Greek Septuagin. version of the Old Testament, and this indicates that his basic training had been obtained outside of Jerusalem and probably outside of Palestine, for the Greek version was not in common use there at that time.

29 What is the second fact?

The author is familiar with the Aramaic language. This is evident from his inclusion of a number of Aramaic words and phrases (5:41; 7:11; 7:34; 14:36; 15:22, 34) which he translates into Greek, as though his readers might not be familiar with their Aramaic form. In only one instance (10:51, where he uses the word "Rabboni") does he allow an Aramaic expression to stand without explanation. This indicates his own knowledge of the language and suggests that he is writing for an audience unfamiliar with it.

30 What is the third fact?

He seems to have had a considerable knowledge of Jewish life and thought. He is generally familiar with conditions and customs in Palestine, but he does not seem to have had such an acquaintanceship as one might have expected from a native son. He is familiar with the larger geographical divisions of Palestine (1:5, 14; 3:8; etc.) but seems to have lacked exact and detailed local information. His statements concerning the movements of Jesus outside of Jerusalem are a bit vague, and at least three geographical errors occur in his account. In one instance (7:31) an impossible route is described; in another (5:1) a territory which lies far south and inland is located on the shore of Galilee; in still another (11:1) the natural order of the villages is reversed. From such facts it might be inferred that what he knew of the land had been learned during visits, or a relatively brief sojourn, in Jerusalem. Also, in certain matters relative to Jewish legal procedure he seems to have been in error, as though he did not have exact and technical information such as would come to a longtime resident of Jerusalem.

31 What, then, is our general impression of Mark?

He seems to have been a Jew who had come into the Christian fellowship as a Hellenist, and to have had only such knowledge

16

of Palestine as an occasional visitor might have gathered. He was at one time the companion of Paul and Barnabas (Acts 15:37), and wrote his Gospel for the Roman Christians.

32 How can we be so confident of that?

For a number of reasons. First of all, of course, there is the testimony of Papias, Irenaeus, and other Church Fathers who declare the book was written in Rome for Roman Christians. Then there is the reference in First Peter (5:13) which locates Mark in Rome ("Babylon"). By various other lines of evidence, including Mark's acceptance of the Roman date for Easter, the belief that the Gospel originated in Rome is well supported, even from the first century.

33 Is the matter of very great importance?

It is of considerable importance, for its composition in Rome will explain many things about the book which would have no explanation on any other basis.

34 For what purpose was the Gospel written?

This is a broad question and one to be studied with care, the answers being dug out of the book itself. First of all, however, let it be said that it was written for Christians who were faced with a very special problem.

35 Why are we so sure it was written for Christians?

Nothing in the book can be considered an appeal to pagans to accept Jesus. If it had been written as an evangelistic tract, it would have contained exhortations, explanations, and appeals directed to nonbelievers, but nothing of the sort appears in Mark's Gospel. It makes no attempt to persuade anyone who may be of a contrary opinion, though it does report numerous controversies. On the other hand, many terms which must have been intelligible to Christians and unintelligible of non-Christians are used without explanation. The author assumes that his readers are familiar with them. Names are introduced without explanation, as though the individuals mentioned were well known to the readers.

36 What was the special problem the Christians faced?

The Neronic persecutions were just subsiding, and the

church at Rome was nursing its wounds. It will be remembered from our study of Revelation that only certain religious groups were recognized by the Roman government, and that Christianity was tolerated only because it was viewed as a Jewish sect. The authorities were suspicious of a new religion. If the Christians could convince them that the new faith was part and parcel of Judaism, trouble might be avoided, for the Jews were allowed religious liberty. Moreover, if the Christians could be inspired to stand up under persecutions, the gospel could be preached to the world. But this depended upon their being thoroughly instructed in the great facts concerning the life and character of their Lord. The Gospel of Mark seems to have been an effort to supply the Christians with these "basics" rather than an attempt to produce a formal "life" of Jesus.

37 Is not the Gospel of Mark a life of Christ?

It cannot be called such for several reasons. In the first place, it makes no attempt to supply a complete record of his life. No reference of any kind is made to his birth, his childhood, his youth, or his family connections, all of which are matters of great interest to a biographer. Instead, the story begins with Jesus as an adult, entering upon his career as a teacher and preacher. Then, once the story is started, long periods of his life are ignored, without a single event thereof being reported. In fact, if all the events which Mark records were added up, they would account for only a few months out of Jesus' total lifetime.

38 What is the Gospel of Mark then?

It is a writing addressed to Christians of the second generation for the purpose of informing them concerning many matters related to the life and teachings of their Lord. Because few of them could have ever seen him when he was alive, and because he taught in Aramaic whereas they spoke Greek, it was highly important that they should be instructed by someone who could speak with some authority.

39 By what authority did Mark speak?

As an individual Mark seems to have been a rather inconspicuous member of the Christian community, but as Peter's assistant he must have enjoyed some prominence. Very naturally anything he said would be listened to with great respect because it would be assumed that he was speaking the mind of Peter. Even though it is impossible to prove that Mark's Gospel is a condensed report of Peter's preaching, it is impossible to escape the conclusion that it carried great weight because of its association with his name.

40 Was the Gospel of Mark written in Greek?

Scholars generally are agreed that it was, though there are some who think it may have been based on Aramaic records. There are even a few who believe that the first Gospel records were composed in Aramaic and translated into Greek, and the debate on this subject is pretty lively among the scholars. But if any Aramaic records ever existed, they have completely disappeared, and we have no real knowledge of them. In the Gospel of Mark we have the most important elements of the Christian belief of about A.D. 75, written in the Greek language of the common people of that time.

41 Was Mark's the first written version of the Christian tradition?

It is the first which could be called reasonably complete, though Mark may have worked with written documents before him. These, however, could have been no more than fragmentary records of individual or isolated events. There is a sense in which Mark's Gospel can be called an innovation.

42 In what respect was it an innovation?

The written record had yet to win its way and establish itself as the standard. In fact, there were those who held all written records under suspicion, preferring the oral tradition. The Jews themselves took great pride in the fact that their interpretations of the Law were memorized, and a part of every Jew's education consisted in committing interpretations to memory. Their entire Old Testament had been brought over from the Hebrew into the Aramaic in memorized form. The story is told of a certain Gamaliel the First (ca. A.D. 50), a famous teacher, who ordered the destruction of a written version of the book of Job on the ground that such a form was an impiety. All this suggests the popularity of the oral form of religious teaching.

43 Do we have any other evidence on this point?

Paul spoke about receiving and passing on the records (I Corinthians 11:23); Acts speaks of remembering "the words of the Lord Jesus" (20:35) and quotes a saying that is not to be found in any Gospel extant; Clement of Rome wrote to the Corinthians about A.D. 95 and quoted sayings of Jesus not found in any of our Gospels; Polycarp of Smyrna did the same thing, referring to "the words of the Lord Jesus."

44 What does all this prove?

It means that there must have been in circulation a very considerable amount of material in oral form which has not been preserved for us, or it can mean that some written material not incorporated in the Gospels preserved to us has passed out of existence. Luke very clearly states (1:1) that he compared records and chose that which he considered important enough to preserve, discarding the rest because it did not suit his purpose.

The thoughtful student will do well to keep in mind the fact that we are here investigating in what may be called a twilight zone, in which the records are incomplete, and that in the absence of exact information we must follow what seem to be the most reasonable assumptions. Yet an argument in support of the dependability of our New Testament records arises from these very conditions.

45 What is that argument in support of our New Testament?

The first-century Christians were honest and sincere people, close to the facts, capable of comparing the written records with the oral tradition. Just because they placed their stamp of approval on the written record, we can accept it as being faithful to the facts and acceptable as a true statement.

46 What was the source of Mark's information?

Aside from Mark's knowledge of the oral tradition, which was the common property of all Christians, Mark had had the advantage of years spent as Peter's secretary-interpreter and must have received much highly important firsthand information concerning Jesus' teachings and activities from the Apostle. Because of the conspicuous place Peter occupies in the narrative, it is easy to believe that the Gospel is composed largely of his memoirs. This becomes even more plausible when we remember that Peter identified himself with the Roman church and that Mark wrote for the Roman Christians. But we shall probably not be far from the facts if we say that Mark consulted some written documents which were circulating in fragmentary form among the Christians, and checked them against the information furnished him by Peter, or against that which had come to him by way of the oral tradition.

47 What portions of Mark may have been derived from documents?

Many believe that the series of controversies is 2:1–3:6 may have been taken from some written document which circulated as a tract among the Christians. Similar in form, and all representing approximately the same viewpoint, they may have been used as a tract in defense of Jesus and his teachings before there was a written Gospel for that purpose. Then in 4:1-34 we have a group of parables which may have constituted a collection gathered up in another little "tract of the times." In 13:5-27 we have a discourse in apocalyptic style which could easily enough have been a tract also—one written to inspire Christians to faithfulness.

48 Does Mark differ greatly from the other Gospels?

The average reader may not notice the differences between Mark and the other three Gospels until his attention is called to them, but then they become quite apparent—differences in both style and content.

49 What is different about Mark's style?

The Gospel of Mark is written in a vigorous, hurried style, as though the author was driven by a great compulsion. The word "immediately" appears forty-eight times; Jesus is represented as living under pressure (6:31); events are piled upon events as though time and space must be conserved.

Considered from the literary standpoint, the style of this Gospel shows many flaws; for the sentences are often either awkward or monotonous in structure (notice how many begin with "And"), and the vocabulary is somewhat limited. Nevertheless there is a certain strength and freshness in the rapid movement, the everyday language of conversation, and the frequent inclusion of picturesque details.

50 What are the characteristics of the content of the Gospel?

There are at least five peculiarities of Mark's Gospel which the careful student should notice: (1) Mark represents Jesus as the Son of God with power. (2) He presents the Christ of controversy. (3) His treatment of Jesus' messiahship is peculiar. (4) His Gospel exalts the idea of martyrdom. (5) It is a book of vigorous faith.

51 What about Jesus as a man of power?

It will be noticed from the outset that Mark is not writing about any ordinary man. He is hardly well launched in his recital of events before he comments on the fact that Jesus impressed his hearers as being a man who spoke with unusual authority (1:22). Then follows immediately a story of a cleansing (1:23-26) which "amazed" the people (1:27) and the healing of Peter's mother-in-law (1:30-31). In the fifth chapter Mark tells of three astounding deeds—the healing of the Gadarene demoniac, the healing of the woman with the issue of blood, and the raising of the daughter of Jairus. Throughout the entire Gospel the miraculous element appears again and again. The careful reader cannot fail to be impressed with the fact that Mark is not trying to present Jesus as an example for man, for obviously no mere human being could hope to duplicate the deeds of Jesus. Rather, the teacher from Galilee is portrayed as the Saviour of men, endowed with astounding power from God.

52 What about the controversies?

If we had no other Gospel than that of Mark, we would get the impression that Jesus was involved in controversy much of the time. There was the question of the forgiveness of sin (2:1-12), of eating with sinners (2:15-17), of fasting (2:18-22), of Sabbath observance (2:23-28), of his own authority (3:22-30), of the ceremonial laws (7:1-16), of divorce (10:2-12), etc. On these and many other matters Jesus was compelled to take issue with the religious leaders of his time, but in Mark's report of the controversies there is a special significance.

53 What is the significance of these controversies?

Three things appear in the account: (1) It is very apparent that the Jewish leaders broke with Jesus over the technicalities of the Law, and that there was nothing they could allege against his character. (2) Many of the controversies seem to have been recorded for the purpose of guiding the Christians of A.D. 70 in moral and spiritual matters. They raged about questions with which the Christians of that time had to deal. (3) Mark seems to have applied the judgments of Jesus to the problems of his Roman readers.

54 How did Mark adapt Jesus' teachings?

We have one special illustration of the fact that Mark adjusted Jesus' teachings to conditions of life in Rome. In Palestine a man might divorce his wife, but the wife had no way in which she could divorce her husband. When Mark recorded Jesus' teachings on divorce, however, he broadened the Master's words on the subject so as to include the women who divorce their husbands (10:2-12). Under the Roman law that was a common occurrence, and Christians who lived under that law needed instruction at that point. Then, in the case of defilement we find something similar again. Jesus had said that the only real defilement was that which came up from within (7:15-21), but Mark suggests that Jesus had pronounced all food clean (7:9), thus solving one of the most vexing problems with which the Gentiles had to deal. From such illustrations it is evident that Mark attempted to bring Jesus' teachings down to date and apply them to the problems which Roman Christians had to face about A.D. 70 in Rome.

55 How did Mark treat the question of Jesus' messiahship?

At the time when Mark wrote his Gospel, the number of Jews who had accepted Jesus was very limited. Most Christians were Gentiles, converted in spite of a big question: If Jesus was the kind of person the Christians declare him to be, why have the

Jews rejected him? Paul had recognized the difficulty of this problem and in his letter to the Romans had tried to explain it by saying that God had hardened their hearts (Romans 9:18). Mark, in one case, suggests that Jesus had taught in parables so that the common people among the Jews might not understand (4:9, 11, 12, 23, 33-34). He says that Jesus openly proclaimed the Kingdom of God but never spoke openly of his own messiahship. When Peter declares his belief in Jesus' divine commission, he is promptly warned to tell no man about it (8:30). Nowhere, until he appears before the high priest, does Jesus declare his own messiahship (14:62). According to Mark it was a strict secret throughout his ministry, up until the time of his trial.

56 What about the idea of martyrdom?

The great theme of Mark's Gospel is the martyrdom of Jesus. Three times it is predicted (10:33; 9:31; 8:31-32), and each time it is connected with the assurance that God will vindicate him. But this calls for disciples who are not afraid of becoming martyrs. Indeed, it is by such suffering that they are to prove their worthiness of beig called to be disciples (10:39).

57 In what respect is Mark's Gospel a book of faith?

We must remember that Mark was writing for a generation of Christians who were hard pressed and who needed much bolstering. But they had at their backs at least a generation of Christian experience upon which to draw. They had seen martyrs die triumphantly, and they had seen the Church spread across the earth in spite of the opposition of the Jews and the persecution of the empire. If the modern student will read the book of Mark against such a backdrop of persecution and suffering, it will suddenly come alive as a great book of faith. It will become a powerful affirmation of the divinity and invincibility of Jesus Christ, the Son of God (1:1). The author is interested in historical facts, of course, but only as they may serve to stimulate faith in Jesus and his way of life.

58 What kind of portrait of Jesus do we get from Mark?

Jesus appears as a very human person in Mark's Gospel. True, he is a miracle worker, but he is no ghostly figure or vague personality. Instead, he is real flesh and blood, full of eagerness and well aware of the forces with which the people have to deal. Mark alone speaks of Jesus as "the carpenter" (6:3), and after reporting him as doing mighty works, being angry, sighing, and confessing ignorance, he records his last words as "Why hast thou forsaken me?" Paul preached a Christ who had become predominantly a heavenly figure, whereas Mark wrote of him as one who walked the earth and shared the life of men.

Though thoroughly human, Jesus was also unusual in a marked degree and entirely apart from ordinary men. The first chapter of Mark's Gospel sets all this out in vivid array. He is the "Son of God" (1:1), more important than John the Baptist (1:7), the "beloved Son" of God (1:11), a man of authority (1:22), and the Holy One of God (1:24). He is the one who was foretold by the prophets (1:2-3), who baptizes with the Holy Spirit (1:8), who receives special visions from heaven (1:10-11), who is attended by angels (1:13), who preaches the gospel of the Kingdom of God (1:15), who has authority to call all men to serve as evangelists of God (1:16-20), who teaches new truths with authority (1:22) who casts out demons (1:25) and heals the sick and leprous (1:31, 40-45), and whose soul is aflame with a missionary passion (1:38-39).

In a time when the Christians were face to face with actual danger, Mark portrays Jesus as a man of intrepid courage. He fears neither demons, lepers, scribes, soldiers, nor the forces of nature. Not even death is able to frighten him, and, though he shrank from the crucifixion, he did not undertake to evade it.

59 How was the Gospel of Mark received?

We have no way of knowing what its reception may have been at the hands of its first readers, though we do know that it has had a most remarkable history. In the first place, it proved so adequate as a statement of the Christian cause that it completely supplanted all the previous records, not one of which has come down to us even in a fragmentary form. In the second place, as we shall see later on in this study, it became the rock base upon which the other Gospels built.

There came a time, however, when the Gospel of Mark was considered less important than the other three. For a good many years it was relegated to a secondary place because Matthew and Luke, for instance, seemed to be so much more complete.

25

Even Augustine (354-430) believed it was a condensation of the Gospel of Matthew. But as scholars began to discover that it was the oldest of the Synoptics and the earliest record of the four Gospels, interest in it began to revive, and many today consider it the most important. There is, however, one extremely interesting fact to be considered relative to the conclusion of the book.

60 What is that interesting fact in its conclusion?

The Gospel of Mark breaks off sharply at 16:8 with a suggestion that more is to follow, which does not, in fact, appear in the book. Instead, the concluding eleven verses seem quite removed from the rest of the text. In several of the oldest manuscripts these last verses 9-20 do not appear at all, and so the Revised Standard Version puts them in a footnote.

61 What does this mean?

The ancient manuscripts were rolled, the last chapter being on the outside, or exposed, portion of the roll. Scholars believe that the end of the roll on which the original, or at least an early, text of Mark was written became worn and broke away, bit by bit, until some of the text was actually destroyed and lost. Then came some earnest and zealous soul who attempted to complete the text by adding the last eleven verses as we have them in the footnote.

62 Is there any proof of this?

The average reader will notice, of course, the sharp break in the text at 16:8. Up to this point there has been a promise that the meeting in Galilee was to be described and the narrative continued beyond the announcement at the tomb. With 16:9, however, the narrative takes an entirely different direction. The two promises of a reunion of Jesus with his disciples in Galilee (14:28 and 16:7) are ignored, and the Gospel of Mark in its present form includes no report of any such reunion. The Gospel of Matthew, however, does provide us with just such a record (Matthew 28:9, 10, 16-20).

Now a comparison of Matthew 28:1-7 with the corresponding section of Mark shows that up to Mark 16:8 Matthew was following Mark very closely. Since the Matthew account fulfills the promise of Mark regarding the reunion in Galilee, it seems reasonable to believe that Matthew's account is taken largely from the original text of Mark. This would mean that Mark was complete when Matthew consulted it but was altered afterward. This conclusion is strengthened by the fact that an Armenian manuscript discovered in 1891 definitely ascribes the last eleven verses of the present Gospel of Mark to a certain "Ariston," who is known to have been one of the disciples who lived before A.D. 130.

63 What does all this mean?

It probably has small significance to the person who reads the New Testament for devotional purposes only, but it has much significance for the thoughtful student. To such it is an indication of the fact that our New Testament has come down to us through a process which makes necessary a scientific and logical investigation of the text by the same methods which are used by students of other literature. Perhaps even more significantly, it introduces us to the very heart of the synoptic problem.

64 What is the Synoptic problem?

Even the most casual reader of the first three Gospels cannot fail to be impressed with the fact that there is a certain amount of material which is common to all. Upon closer investigation we discover that all but about forty verses or passages of Mark are contained in either Matthew or Luke. In other words, if Mark had perished entirely as an independent writing, all but forty passages would have been preserved in the other two Gospels.

Both Matthew and Luke contain much material besides that of Mark. When we study this additional material with care, we discover that it falls into three classes: (1) some which is common to both Matthew and Luke, (2) some which is found only in Matthew, and (3) some which is found only in Luke.

The question immediately arises as to the relationships of the three Gospels. What, for instance, explains the fact that some material is common to all? Why do Matthew and Luke run parallel in other material which is not included in Mark's Gospel? What is the meaning of the independent material in Matthew and Luke? Where did any of the Gospel writers get the material originally? The long series of questions arising from these facts constitute what is known among scholars as the Synoptic question, or the Synoptic problem.

65 What does "synoptic" mean?

The meaning of the word is "viewed together," and, when applied to the three Gospels, it means that, because they present a common synopsis or outline of Jesus' life, they are to be considered as a unit, each one telling the story from a slightly different angle.

66 Where do we begin with our study of the problem?

We begin with the fact that all the Gospels deal with the same general theme—the life and teachings of Jesus of Nazareth. Under such circumstances certain duplications would be inevitable. No one, for instance, could deal with the life of Abraham Lincoln and omit the fact that he was assassinated. Nor could any writer deal with the life of Jesus and omit all reference to the crucifixion. But the events of Jesus' life, alone, do not tell the whole story. The Master was a great teacher; no one could discuss his life and ignore his teachings.

This means that two types of material appear in all the Gospels—narrative and discourse. The narrative is the record of events connected with the life of Jesus, and the discourses report our Lord's teaching and preaching.

67 What does this reveal?

In the Gospel of Mark the narrative material predominates by a wide margin. The Greek text consists of 11,000 words, in round numbers, of which 7,000 are narrative. In the case of Matthew there are 18,500 words, of which 8,000 are narrative. Luke consists of 21,000 words, of which 9,250 are narrative. It therefore appears that Matthew contains only about 1,000 and Luke 2,250, more words of narrative than Mark.

A comparison of Mark with the other two reveals the fact that neither Matthew nor Luke adds very much to the narrative furnished by the second Gospel. Furthermore, in all cases in which the three are parallel there is remarkable agreement. Matthew and Luke will always be found in general agreement with Mark, but in those cases in which they are reporting some fact not found in Mark they often disagree.

68 Give a specific case.

The Nativity stories are an excellent illustration. Mark makes no mention of Jesus' birth but opens his account with a report of the activity of John the Baptist. Matthew and Luke, on the other hand, give considerable space to accounts of the advent of our Lord (Matthew 1–2; Luke 1:1–2:40), and even a hurried reading of the two makes it plain that they differ widely. Luke, for instance, makes no mention of the visit of the wise men, while Matthew says nothing of the visit of the shepherds nor of the birth of John the Baptist. Except for the similarity of names, one might think he was reading two entirely different stories. In Matthew's account Mary is a very inconspicuous person but in Luke she is the principal actor.

69 Why does Mark make no mention of Jesus' birth?

It is impossible to answer this question, for Mark provides us with no clue. The best we can do is to approximate an answer on the basis of a few known facts.

70 What is the approximate answer?

The Gospel of Mark was written for the Roman Christians, who were Gentiles. A very great deal of their knowledge of the Christian faith had come to them through Peter and Paul. We know from reading Paul's letters that the doctrine of the virgin birth did not occupy much of his thinking, for he makes no mention of it in any way. If the Pauline letters in the New Testament are typical of Paul's preaching, then we must conclude that he laid little emphasis upon the doctrine if, indeed, he preached it at all. In other words, if we had no other New Testament than Paul's letters, we would never have heard of the virgin birth.

If we are correct in assuming that Mark drew a large part of his information from Peter, then the fact that his Gospel makes no mention of the virgin birth would indicate that Peter gave the matter little attention, if any at all. This would indicate that the Nativity stories were not widely reported among the Roman Christians. They seem to have built up their faith and their church independently of this great doctrine. The early missionary preaching was confined to discussions of Jesus' public ministry (Acts 1:21-22), with the resurrection as the great central fact.

It appears that both had copies of Mark's Gospel before them as they wrote, and that both included the bulk of Mark's work (fifteen-sixteenths of Mark appears in Matthew) and added other material as it might suit their special purposes.

72 Is there any proof of this?

Let us compare Mark 13:14 with Matthew 24:15-16. Here are two passages almost identical so far as the statement of fact is concerned. But there is also in each case a comment in parenthesis, and even these comments are identical in the two verses. Note, also, that the comment is inserted at the same place in both cases. It is very difficult to believe that both writers accidentally inserted the same comment at the same place. It is much easier to believe that one copied from the other.

Compare Mark 6:14, 16-17 with Matthew 14:1-3. Here we have accounts of the death of John the Baptist which are almost identical in phrasing and *out of historical order in both cases*. Mark 1:16 and Matthew 4:18 are two more passages that parallel with the explanatory statement "For they were fishermen"—identical in phraseology and order. Mark 3:19, Matthew 10:4, and Luke 6:16 all refer to Judas as a traitor and all tell that he was "one of the twelve" (Matthew 26:14; Mark 14:10; Luke 22:3). In Mark 5:24, Matthew 9:19, and Luke 8:42 we have the story of Jairus' daughter cut off at the same point and the story of the woman with the issue of blood introduced in the same way, all three Gospels agreeing in the statement that she had been afflicted for twelve years. The most reasonable explanation in all cases is that copying has been done.

Mark 1:32, Matthew 8:16, and Luke 4:40 furnish an even more dramatic illustration in support of the theory of copying. In this case Mark uses two expressions to indicate that the day is done—"evening" and "at sundown." Matthew has copied "evening," and Luke has copied "when the sun was setting."

Other passages which will repay some study are Mark 2:8-11, Matthew 9:2-8, and Luke 5:22-24, with special attention to the comment and parenthesis. Then there is the story of the healing of the withered hand (Mark 3:4-6; Matthew 12:12-14; Luke 6:9-11), the healing of the demoniac of the tombs (Mark 5:1-20; Matthew 8:28-34; Luke 8:26-39), Herod's anxiety (Mark 6:14-16;

Matthew 14:1-2; Luke 9:7-9), and the feeding of the multitude (Mark 6:35-44; Matthew 14:15-21; Luke 9:12-17).

73 How do these similarities raise a problem?

It is easy to see that the three Gospels are closely related. They are all telling many of the same facts. But three writers, working independently, would not be apt to use the same identical words or parallel their recitals so closely unless there were some sort of collaboration between them. The honest Bible student wants to know what that collaboration was. The explanation of so conspicuous a fact is extremely important to any intelligent understanding of the Gospel story.

74 Are they not three reports of the same facts?

It is true that the Synoptic Gospels are all reporting the same events, but we must remember that they are not eyewitness reports. Rather, they are reports formulated at least fifty years after the events.

If three newspaper reporters wrote an account of a fire, each being present, it would be inevitable that certain basic facts would be the same in all reports—the location, the time, the extent of the damage. Each would tell the story as he saw it, but they would not be apt to use the same identical words and phrases. If three historians undertook to write the story of the fire fifty years after it had occurred and we discovered that whole sentences and even paragraphs were repeated verbatim in two or more of the reports, we would conclude that all three had copied from some common source. But if we then discovered that almost the total of one account was included in the other two, with the exact order of statement maintained in numerous instances, we would naturally conclude that one of the reports was the original and that the other two had drawn upon it for material.

This is exactly the process by which scholars have reasoned in the case of the Synoptics. They have discovered that the Gospel of Mark appears almost entirely in Matthew and Luke. Moreover, they have discovered that these two books follow the same order as in Mark when using Mark's material. For these and other reasons it has been agreed by practically all scholars that Mark is the earliest Gospel and that the other two—Matthew and Luke—have drawn upon it for their basic material.

75 Could not Mark have borrowed from the other two?

It is difficult to believe that Mark borrowed from Matthew or Luke; for they contain considerable additional material, and, if he had been borrowing, it seems incredible that he would have omitted anything so significant and important as the birth stories and the Sermon on the Mount. Then there is a considerable list of very great parables in Matthew and Luke which Mark does not mention. Surely he would not have ignored these if he had been copying.

76 What are we to conclude then?

Scholars of practically all shades of opinion are generally agreed that Mark is the oldest of the three Gospels and that Matthew and Luke depended upon it for their basic material. When they quote Mark, they adhere closely to his version, altering it only to improve its style or to add some personal comment.

77 Do we have any proof of this?

In Luke's very first verse he confesses to having consulted the works of others. While he does not name Mark as one of his sources, we are justified in assuming he did consult the second Gospel when we find long passages from it embedded in the Gospel of Luke.

78 Does Matthew make any such confession?

There is no intimation in the Gospel of Matthew as to the source of the material, but, since the process is plainly described in Luke and the same results are apparent in Matthew, we may assume that the latter followed Luke's procedure.

79 Does this explain all of Matthew and Luke?

By no means. Both Gospels contain much that has not been drawn from Mark at all. This presents an additional problem.

80 What is this new problem?

Just as we discovered a marked similarity between Mark and extensive passages in Matthew and Luke, so we discover certain

32

very evident similarities between the first and third Gospels.

81 Of what does this material consist?

It would require too much space to list the entire body of material contained in Matthew and Luke in common, and the student is referred to any good "harmony" of the Gospels in which the parallel passages are printed in adjoining columns. For an excellent discussion of the entire Synoptic problem, including exhaustive scripture citations the student is referred to "The Structure of the Synoptic Gospels," by Professor E. W. Burch, in the *Abingdon Bible Commentary.* A careful study of all the material common to the two, and not found in Mark, reveals at least two very interesting facts.

82 What is the first interesting fact?

We discover that the material, in very large part, consists of discourses of Jesus rather than reports of his activities. The student will recall that in Mark we read chiefly about actions, movements, and events in Jesus' life. Matthew and Luke are dependent almost entirely upon Mark for their information in this field. But the material drawn from outside of Mark deals, in very large part, with Jesus' teachings and public addresses.

83 What is the second interesting fact?

The two Gospels follow different orders and arrangements of their material, even though the actual phrases are closely parallel in the two versions. In this connection we come upon a very interesting fact concerning the activities of our Lord.

84 What is so interesting about his activities?

Because none of the Gospel writers attempted to produce a real biography of Jesus, the New Testament lacks precise information at many points. No exact date for his birth is given, for instance. Many details have to be approximated for lack of exact information. According to the most careful studies, the ministry of Jesus must have lasted for at least 550 days, and perhaps longer, but on the basis of all the New Testament records we are able to identify no more than five weeks of activity at the most. Mark fixes no more than thirty-one days of activity (1:9-13; 1:14-20; 1:21-34; 1:35-38; 1:39-45; 2:1-22; 2:23-3:6;

3:7-19*a*; 3:19*b*-4:41; 5:1-20; 5:21-43; 6:1-6*a*; 6:7-13; 6:30-52; 6:53–7:23; 7:24-30; 7:31-37; 8:1-10; 8:11-26; 8:27–9:1; 9:2-29; 9:33-50; 10:1-31; 10:32-45; 10:46-52; 11:1-11; 11:12-19; 11:20-33; 14:1-11; 14:12-52; 14:53–15:47). All we know about the life of Jesus has come from those thirty-one days. For the student with imagination, this fact will be thrilling. Thirty-one days of one life have changed the course of the world's history!

85 What is the explanation for the similarity in Matthew and Luke?

We must remind ourselves that in the two Gospels there are two kinds of material which are similar. There is the Marcan material, which has already been studied. Then there is the "discoursive material" which is found in the two Gospels and not found in Mark. This, like the material from Mark, seems to have been lifted from some common source.

86 Do we know of any such common source?

There is an old tradition to the effect that Matthew, one of our Lord's disciples, wrote down a series of sayings which he had chosen from the Master's sermons. These were called the "Logia," or "Sayings," and Papias, to whom we have referred several times in these studies, says that they owed their origin to Matthew, who compiled them in Aramaic. He called them "oracles," though the exact meaning of that word as he used it is not quite clear. Many scholars doubt details of Papias' report for various reasons; it is impossible to go into the matter at length in our limited space. But we can conclude at least one thing.

87 What can we conclude about the two Gospels?

Even though we are not able to identify the author, there seems to have been at least one written source besides Mark available to both Matthew and Luke, and there may have been several. Luke says he consulted more than one, and it is reasonable to assume that many of those available to Luke were also available to the compiler of Matthew's Gospel. At any rate many of the sayings, parables, etc., are duplicated in both Gospels in a form that indicates that both authors copied them from an earlier document. To this document the scholars have given a name.

88 What is that name?

Because of their inability to identify the unknown document, or documents, from which Matthew and Luke copied, scholars have called it the "Q document." The German word for "source" is *Quelle,* and the "Q" document means simply the "source document."

89 What do we know about the Q document?

We know nothing about who wrote it, how extensive it was, nor when it was written. But since the duplicated material in Matthew and Luke consists almost entirely of discourses and comments of Jesus, it is believed that it was a document containing extracts from his teachings. The only events reported may have been the baptism, the temptation, and the encounter with the centurion of Capernaum. For our purposes it is sufficient to say that Q must have been a compilation of the more important sayings of Jesus to which Matthew and Luke were both deeply indebted.

90 Is Q entirely incorporated in Matthew and Luke?

We have noted that Mark is almost entirely incorporated into Matthew and Luke, but in the case of Q we cannot be sure. Beyond the duplicated material already noted, which by definition comes from Q, it is quite possible that Matthew quoted material from Q which Luke did not consider sufficiently important to incorporate into his Gospel, and vice versa. Thus it may be true that both Matthew and Luke used portions of Q which the other did not. However, it cannot be determined positively that the "independent" material of the two Gospels came, even in part, from Q.

91 What is our final judgment?

We can proceed on a belief that at least four things are true:
1. Both Matthew and Luke copied from Mark.
2. Both Matthew and Luke copied from Q.
3. Matthew includes some material, not found in Mark or Luke, which may have come from Q, and other material which came from a source used only by Matthew.
4. Luke includes some material, not found in Mark or Matthew, which may have come from Q, and other material

besides which came from a source used only by Luke.

92 **How many documents are there in the Gospel material?**

It is impossible to answer that question. In the case of the Old Testament we identified at least four—J, E, P, D—but in the New Testament the evidence is not so clear. Luke says very clearly that he consulted many (1:1). It is sufficient for our purpose to say that the Synoptic Gospels used at least two—Mark and Q—and probably several others.

93 **Did they use both in the same way?**

When Matthew and Luke copied from Mark, they preserved both the words and the order, but they seem to have treated Q more liberally. The purposes of the two writers being different, it is natural that they should use the material differently, according to their own designs.

94 **What was the difference?**

Matthew, as we shall see, attempted to prove that Jesus was the long-looked-for Messiah of the Jews, and he used Jesus' discourses to support that theme. Luke, on the other hand, affirms his purpose in the very first verses (1:1-3) of his book and says he has attempted "to write an orderly account." In other words, he professes to be a historian, whereas Matthew makes no such claim for himself.

95 **Does not this throw the New Testament into confusion?**

It may seem so to the student who comes in contact with these facts for the first time, but as he meditates upon them it will soon begin to clarify much that has previously puzzled him. On the other hand, it all constitutes one of the strongest arguments for the reliability of our New Testament record.

96 **How does it prove the New Testament's reliability?**

The Synoptic Gospels were all written within seventy years of the time Jesus was crucified. The entire Christian community throughout the earth had at least some knowledge of the facts concerning the life and activity of Jesus. Just as it would be impossible for any American to write a life of Abraham Lincoln today which distorted the basic facts concerning him, so it would have been impossible for the Gospel writers to have seriously misrepresented Jesus. There is, however, one great difference: a biography of Mr. Lincoln is a purely private venture, but the Gospels were public works in which the Christian community had an interest and a stake. If a biography of Lincoln assumed to be an "official" version of the president's career, it would have to come under some sort of official scrutiny and meet some official approval. In the case of the Gospels, they became "official" by the process of common acceptance among the Christians. They began as private ventures, but because of their fidelity they were finally elevated to the dignity of being called "inspired."

If the Synoptic Gospels, composed between A.D. 70 and A.D. 90, had had no other authority behind them than the authority of their individual authors, their claim upon our credulity would be limited. They have that, of course, but they have more. It can be said that the Synoptic Gospels represent what the Christian Church of A.D. 70-100 believed to be true concerning Jesus and his teachings. They were preserved by the Church as an accurate and faithful report of the life and teachings of Jesus; they were subjected to the scrutiny of the entire Christian movement and survived because they were judged to be authentic. Had there been any element of fraud in them, that would have been detected and they would have been repudiated. This simple fact throws an entirely new light upon the dependability of our New Testament.

97 What is that new light?

We can now accept our New Testament with an entirely new confidence. In the first place, the oral tradition was the fruitage of the reports given to the Christian Church by the disciples and others who had seen Jesus in the flesh. In the second place, such written records as there may have been had to stand the test of the scrutiny of living witnesses in order to survive. As time went on a certain body of information became common throughout the Church—information which was searched, scrutinized, examined, and tested. When the Synoptic Gospels took form, they had to conform in all their essentials to the oral tradition throughout the Church, and to any accredited writings which may have then existed. The fact that the three Synoptic Gospels, widely read and examined by the Church within no more than seventy years following the resurrection of Jesus, were accepted by Christians everywhere and preserved in their present form with such meticulous care, means that they have back of them more than the authority of the individual authors.

98 What is that additional authority?

In a very real sense it may be said that the Synoptic Gospels are the certified account of the life and teachings of Jesus—an account which has back of it the moral and spiritual approval of the entire first-century Christian Church. The Christians who lived within fifty years of Jesus himself—probably many of the older Christians were even closer in point of time—preserved the Synoptic Gospels because they were true and dependable accounts. They therefore have back of them the authority of the Church itself. There is a sense in which it can be said that the entire Christian Church authored them. Particular statements as they have come down to us may prove to be erroneous in matters of geography, chronology, etc. But the basic elements, teachings, facts, and events can be accepted as having been reliably reported.

99 Which Gospel was written following Mark?

It is impossible to prove positive statements in the case, for there could not have been much time between the compiling of Matthew and Luke, though the preponderance of opinion favors the judgment that Matthew was the next Gospel to take form.

100 What is the Gospel of Matthew?

It is the Gospel which has stood at the head of the collection of four Gospels in every New Testament we have ever had. Although it is not the oldest of the four, it has enjoyed some pre-eminence because it bore the name of a disciple (as did John's Gospel also), but more particularly because it is the most complete statement of the Gospel case, because it contains large teaching sections, and because it is presented in a popular fashion.

101 When was the Gospel of Matthew written?

There seem to be several allusions in the Gospel of Matthew to the fall of Jerusalem. This occurred A.D. 70, and is the first fact which may serve to guide us in fixing its date of composition. That it is so obviously dependent upon Mark's Gospel, which was written about A.D. 65 to 70, is a second fact that will assist us. If we settle then, on about A.D. 80, we cannot be far from the right date.

102 What did the fall of Jerusalem have to do with Matthew's Gospel?

The most difficult question the Christians had to answer was, "Why do not the Jews accept their Messiah?" This was apt to be one of the first questions an intelligent and thoughtful Gentile would ask. If Jesus was all the Christians claimed for him, they were saying it certainly was strange that the Jews should have repudiated him, even to the point of demanding his death at the hands of a Roman governor.

In A.D. 70 the Jewish capital city, Jerusalem, was destroyed as a result of a revolt on the part of the Jews. In the course of the struggle the most awful horrors were witnessed inside the city, an account of which is to be found in Josephus' *Wars of the Jews*. The destruction of the beloved city, together with its Temple and sacred places, produced a profound effect upon the Jewish communities scattered throughout the empire and raised serious religious problems for Jews everywhere. Although the Jews had enjoyed many favors through many years as a result of the diplomacy of Herod the Great, Rome was no longer sure of their loyalty anywhere.

The fall of Jerusalem seemed to answer at least one question for the Christians. They believed that the Jewish nation, in repudiating Jesus as its Messiah, had lost the right to call itself the chosen of God. They believed that the blessings of the covenant had passed from the Jewish nation to the Christian Church. This, in their opinion, was the true Israel henceforth, and there were those who looked upon the destruction of Jerusalem as evidence of God's final abandonment of the Jewish nation as the chosen people. It was common for the Jews to present an argument in the form of a narrative (Acts 7:1-53; 11:1-18; 13:16-41), and in some such way Matthew may have attempted to argue the case of Jesus' messiahship.

103 How did Matthew solve the problem?

He believed profoundly that Jesus was the Messiah of the Jews, long and often promised by the prophets. He had offered himself to the nation and it had rejected him, thereby bringing down upon itself the wrath of Jehovah. It had been offered the Kingdom of Heaven and had lost its chance. Thereafter the good news of the Kingdom was for the Greeks, and not for the Jews except as they were willing to come into the Kingdom as any other aliens would. This, in turn, represented a very great assumption on the part of the Christians.

104 What did the Christians assume?

One of the basic doctrines of the Jews was that they had been chosen by God for special favors, to be messengers, and to be the medium through which the world was to receive any redemption for which it might ever hope. The Christians came to the belief that when the Jews rejected Jesus the Christian movement inherited the promises made to Israel and became the true Israel. This doctrine was studied in connection with the Fourth Gospel and the Revelation. Naturally such an assumption could not fail to create a bitter rivalry between the Christians and the Jews.

105 How did Matthew undertake to prove his case?

He set out to write a life of Jesus which would prove his point. Beginning at his birth and proceeding on down to his resurrection, the author undertook to show that Jesus fulfilled Hebrew prophecy concerning the Messiah. Sixteen times we find the word "fulfill" in the Gospel of Matthew (1:22; 2:15; 2:17; 2:23; 3:15; 4:14; 5:17; 8:17; 12:17; 13:14; 13:35; 21:4; 26:54; 26:56; 27:9; 27:35). In some instances the references are a bit strained, and in other cases actually inaccurate, but the complete argument must have been very impressive in that day.

106 Why should it have been so impressive?

Because the method of proof-text interpretation which Matthew uses was extremely popular with the Jews at that time. It was used over and over by the rabbis of that century as they undertook to prove their doctrines according to their law. Among Christians and Jews it was the accepted form of argument.

107 What mistakes did Matthew make?

In one case (27:9) he ascribes a prophecy to Jeremiah which is actually from Zechariah (11:13). In another instance (23:35) he refers to Zechariah, son of Barachiah, as having been slain between the sanctuary and the altar, when an entirely different man was the victim. In still another case, in connection with his genealogies, he omits three kings from the list (Ahaziah, Jehoash, and Amaziah—II Kings 8:25; 12:1; 14:1-2), though their reigns totaled seventy years.

108 What about those genealogies?

Alongside their doctrine of the Messiah, a belief had grown up among the Jews that no Messiah was genuine who did not descend from David. This appears several times in the New Testament (Acts 2:30 ff.; 13:22-23; Romans 1:3; II Timothy 2:8; Revelation 22:16), though Jesus himself dismissed the idea rather lightly (Matthew 22:43-45).

The Gospel of Matthew undertakes to show that Jesus descended from David according to the popular expectation. But it goes even farther back and traces Jesus' ancestry through to Abraham. There are three divisions—Abraham to David (1:2-6a), David to the Babylonian Exile (1:6b-11), and the Babylonian captivity to Joseph the husband of Mary (1:12-16). Each division has fourteen names, among which are those of four women—a very unusual thing in Hebrew genealogies—which some have interpreted to mean that Jesus was to minister to women in some special way. It is of additional interest to note that all the women were foreigners and, with the exception of Ruth, sinners.

109 What is the meaning of the genealogies?

The implication of Matthew's genealogies is that all of Jewish history has led up to Jesus, and that through him the broken fortunes of Israel are to be restored and redeemed. The bright hopes which the prophets held out to the Hebrews are to be realized in Jesus and his ministry. He is to usher in a new kingdom in which all that is noblest and holiest in men will finally be realized. In a word, the author is attempting to preach the belief that there is a holy and divine design in history, of which Jesus is the culmination. But it must be admitted that his genealogy raises some very difficult questions.

110 What are those difficulties?

First of all, Matthew's genealogy does not agree with Luke's (3:23-38), and all attempts to reconcile the two have failed thus far. Both tables seem to be incomplete, and to clear them up is a fruitless endeavor. Even if we were able to do so, the results would hardly justify the effort.

In the second place, the genealogical table seems to cancel the story of the virgin birth. If Jesus' descent was by way of Joseph's line, then the doctrine of Jesus' messiahship would be strengthened in the eyes of the Jews, for Joseph's line ran back to David. But Matthew's account of the advent of Jesus furnishes one of the strongest arguments in behalf of the doctrine of the virgin birth; his report divorces Jesus from Joseph's line and ascribes his birth, through the miracle, to Mary's line alone. This brings out the fact that in the New Testament we have at least three different and distinct explanations of the unique personality of Jesus.

111 What are those three explanations?

1. In Mark's Gospel we are told that at the time of Jesus' baptism he became the medium through which the Spirit of God was manifested to mankind (Mark 1:4-11).

2. In the Fourth Gospel (1:1-18) and in Paul's letter to the Philippians (2:5-8) it is declared that Jesus had existed as a divine being long before he ever came to dwell on earth with men.

3. In Matthew and Luke it is said that Jesus was born of a virgin as a direct result of an act of the Spirit of God.

112 What are we to conclude from all this?

The brief limits of this study make it impossible to follow this question of the virgin birth out to all its implications. We know at least four things, however, and when these have been stated

42

we can well proceed to other matters.

1. The report of the virgin birth as it appears in Matthew and the corresponding report as it appears in Luke are by no means identical. Matthew's is Joseph-centered and Luke's is Mary-centered.

2. Paul, the first to produce any Christian writings, makes no reference to the matter. The Fourth Gospel, which was the supreme effort of a great thinker to interpret Jesus to the thoughtful Greek world, makes no mention of the doctrine and offers no facts of any kind concerning any unusual circumstances attending Jesus' birth.

3. It is admitted by practically all scholars that the story of the miraculous birth was not preached by the Christian Church until a relatively late date.

4. Jesus himself, according to any reliable account available to us, makes no reference to the matter in any way, directly or indirectly.

From these four facts it seems evident that neither Jesus nor Paul required a belief in this doctrine on the part of any who proposed to call themselves Christians. Just when people were asked to believe in it is not known definitely.

113 Who wrote the Gospel of Matthew?

As in several other instances, the question of authorship cannot be settled. For many years it was assumed that the book was written by Matthew, one of our Lord's disciples, but that cannot be proved. The student must have noticed that the text itself offers no comment of any kind upon the subject—it remains altogether anonymous. Whatever we are able to decide in the matter must be based on statements outside the New Testament, together with whatever evidence we are able to piece together from the text itself.

114 How was Matthew's name attached to the book?

Eusebius, the historian, quotes Papias, the bishop of Hierapolis, as saying, "So Matthew composed the oracles [logia] in the Hebrew language and each one translated them as he could." This probably refers to a collection of sayings, teachings, texts, or fragmentary notes, which was used in instructing new converts to Christianity. For many years it was believed that the First Gospel was an expanded form of these "logia," and scholars used to refer to the original as "The Sayings of Matthew." More recent scholarship has adopted the name "Q," as has been explained (Question 88). Certainly neither Q nor the Sayings of Matthew could have been the Gospel of Matthew in its present form. It is entirely possible that the author of the Gospel may have had some connection with the Logia of Matthew, but of that we have neither proof nor disproof. The fact is, however, that the name of Matthew has been attached to the Gospel from the earliest times.

115 Who was Matthew?

By profession Matthew belonged to the most despised class in the land—the tax collectors. According to the Roman practice, the responsibility for collecting the imperial revenues was farmed out to individuals who offered the highest bid for the privilege. Then they reimbursed themselves by collecting "what the traffic would bear." Matthew was stationed at Capernaum, where the tolls were levied on all caravans of merchandise that traveled along the road leading to Damascus. It was a very lucrative post (Luke 19:2) and probably cost him a pretty penny, for Rome was not accustomed to appointing men to such positions without first securing a generous cash guarantee which corresponded somewhat to a modern bond. On the occasion of being invited to become one of Jesus' disciples Matthew gave a great feast in celebration of the event (Luke 5:29 f.) and thereafter forsook his business (Luke 5:28) and became a disciple. His original name seems to have been Levi (Mark 2:14; Luke 5:27) but upon becoming a member of the band of disciples he became known as Matthew ("gift of God") and continued to be known by that name among the Christians (Matthew 9:9). Tradition has it that he preached for some fifteen years in Judea, following the resurrection, and then visited Ethiopia, Persia, Media, and Parthia.

116 Could Matthew have written the Gospel?

It is possible that he may have had some part in compiling it, and may actually have written down some notes which became the core of the book, but we have already noted that the basic information comes from Mark's Gospel. It would seem very strange for Matthew, a disciple of Jesus, to have depended upon Mark's account, even though he was Peter's secretary; for surely Matthew would consider his own information on most points as reliable as that of Peter.

In the second place, we have seen that there is a large section of Matthew which corresponds very closely to Luke's account. Papias says that Matthew's logia were in Aramaic, and scholars are agreed that our Gospel of Matthew is not a translation into Greek but a work originally composed in Greek. Because of the form in which the material appears, it is the belief of most scholars that the first Gospel is the work of a compiler who worked with both written documents and the oral tradition, and who fashioned his record according to his purpose out of materials already existing in large part.

It is a fact, of course, that Matthew was an officer of the Roman government, or at least a professional man of sorts. It seems reasonable to believe that he was skilled in the art of writing, but that must remain no more than a very likely assumption, for we have no positive proof. At most he could have written no more than a small portion of the book which we now know as "the Gospel of Matthew." In spite of the fact that we cannot positively identify the author by name, however, there are a few things we can say about him.

117 What do we know about the author?

There seem to be good reasons for believing that he was a Jew who lived outside of Palestine. He appears to have been well versed in the Jewish scriptures, but in all those instances in which he quotes from the Old Testament he uses the Greek, or Septuagint, version. This would be expected of a Hellenist Jew, whereas a Jew of Palestine might have been expected to quote from the original Hebrew.

He was fully convinced that Jesus fulfilled the conditions predicted of the Messiah by the prophets, but he was well aware that he had not fulfilled the popular expectations of a Messiah. It became his task, therefore, to show that those expectations were mistaken in some part but that, though the messianic mission of Jesus was different from the popular expectation, it was messianic nevertheless. Paul had wrestled with this same problem in his letter to the Romans (chaps. 9-11).

118 Where was the Gospel of Matthew written?

Christianity had failed to win a great following among the

Jews, but it was succeeding gloriously among the Gentiles when Matthew was written. It was in the city of Antioch in Syria, that the disciples were first called "Christians" (Acts 11:26). For a time it appeared that Antioch might become the great central city of the Christian movement, though that honor finally passed to Ephesus. A strong Christian congregation continued there for many years. It is very interesting to discover that Ignatius, the bishop of Antioch, quoted from the first Gospel in one of his early works, and that in that city the first mission to the Greeks was organized (Acts 14:26-27; 15:35-41). There is no positive proof that the Gospel of Matthew was written at Antioch, but there is a widespread opinion among scholars that this may have been so.

119 What are their reasons?

The Antioch church seems to have been the meeting ground of Jewish and Gentile influences (Acts 6:5; 11:19-20, 26-27; 15:22-30). On two occasions the author speaks of something as having continued "to this day" (27:8; 28:15), implying that some time had elapsed to allow the movement to get under way. There was keen disappointment among the Christians at the close of the first century that Jesus had not made his second appearance, and this is hinted in a way that would have sounded natural in Antioch (24:48; 25:5). Persecutions are referred to (5:11; 10:18; 25:36, 39), and with these the Christians of Antioch must have been familiar. Peter had been associated with the church at Antioch (Galatians 2:11), and in the Gospel of Matthew we have at least two stories about that disciple which are not to be found in any other Gospel—walking on the water (Matthew 14:24-32) and the promise of the rock (Matthew 16:18). Some believe these may have been stories told of Peter in and about Antioch.

120 How did the author proceed with his book?

For the sake of convenience, from this point on we shall speak of the author of the first Gospel as Matthew, even though we have seen that the disciple of that name could have been no more than a partial author of the Gospel.

As we go into the material of the book itself, we discover that the author has a fixed and simple plan for presenting his argument and material. There is an explanatory or introductory section, consisting of the Nativity story (chaps. 1-2), which seems to have come from some independent source. At least we have nothing like it anywhere else in the New Testament.

Then follows a large body of material consisting of twenty-three chapters, which falls naturally into five divisions and which reminds us of the five divisions of the Jewish Book of the Law, each of which consists of a narrative section and a composite teaching section.

Finally there is the resurrection story, consisting of three chapters (26-28), which is based on Mark's account. There are, however, certain additional episodes of a wonderful nature (26:53 f.; 27:24, 51-54; 28:2) which may have been drawn from an additional record, sometimes called hypothetically a "wonder book."

As a result of its structure the Gospel of Matthew was considered almost ideal for use in instructing the converts to Christianity. It was valued because (1) it is conveniently arranged, (2) it contains an extended statement of the teachings of Jesus, and (3) it presents the most comprehensive portrait of Christ which we have in the New Testament.

Because the author seems to have the Church in mind at all times, being the only one of the four Gospel writers who mentions it, there are those who think that Matthew was written about A.D. 90, or ten years later than Luke. Its theological development lends weight to this belief.

121 What about the Nativity story?

Mention has already been made of the fact that it differs greatly from the Nativity story in Luke. It tells about the wise men, for instance, as if astrology had come to pay tribute to the superior personality and message of Jesus. We know that astrology exercised a strong influence in Antioch. Just as the author of John's Gospel was under the necessity of showing that the Baptist had been superseded by Jesus, so Matthew had to show that astrology and kindred superstitions had been superseded by the Christian faith and the Christian interpretation of the universe.

122 What about the five divisions of Matthew's Gospel?

This material is included in chapters three to twenty-five, and each section concludes with words such as "When Jesus had finished these sayings." The plan is uniform throughout the five divisions; each has a narrative followed by a discourse.

1. The first division consists of chapters three through seven.
2. The second includes chapters eight through 11:1.
3. The third extends from 11:2 through 13:53.
4. The fourth is 14:1 through 18:35.
5. The fifth is made up of chapters 19-25.

123 What is the basic message of the first division?

To the Jews, the figure of Moses filled the whole horizon. He was the lawgiver, the first great leader of the nation, and its final moral and religious authority. On the mountain he had been given the tables of the Law which became the great charter of the nation (Exodus 19:20).

To the Christians, Jesus was the final authority. His words were to be law, and his teachings were to be the basic code for all men. Matthew therefore sets out to establish Jesus' position as the "Moses of Christianity." He recites a series of incidents calculated to portray him as one who has been divinely chosen—his baptism at the hands of John the Baptist (3:1-17), which linked him to the popular prophet of the desert whose preaching had been such a sensation; his temptation (4:1-11), which established him as a divine person and a trustworthy leader; the calling of his disciples (4:12-25) and the launching of his crusade for the Kingdom. With this kind of preliminary narrative, Matthew is ready to present his first great body of teachings, known as the Sermon on the Mount.

124 What is the Sermon on the Mount?

It is an outline of the ethical ideals of Christianity. It gets its name from the fact that Matthew represents it as an address delivered to the disciples on a mountainside, but it could hardly have been a formal deliverance prepared as a sermon. Rather, it seems to have been a collection of choice sayings of Jesus culled from many conversations and speeches. The same material is to be found scattered through the Gospel of Luke, a bit here and a bit there. The reader will notice that it is not an elaboration of any particular theme, but a series of epigrammatic assertions of a religious and ethical nature which elaborate the concept of the righteousness of the Kingdom of Heaven. Perhaps the most conspicuous single section is that known as the Beatitudes (5:1-12). The Gospel of Luke also contains a series of Beatitudes (6:20-26), but they are in no way so impressive as the Matthew version, though they do furnish us with a hint as to Matthew's method of composition.

125 What about Matthew's composition?

It seems to have been the case that Matthew had before him a document containing many of Jesus' sayings and teachings in concise form. What this document may have been we cannot know, but from its contents he seems to have selected material according to the theme with which he was dealing. In the case of the narrative material which he borrowed from Mark, he deviated very little from either the form or the order of the original, but both Matthew and Luke rearranged the discourse material to suit their own purposes.

126 What is the basic message of the second section?

The second section, like the first, consists of a series of incidents (8:1–9:36) marshaled for the purpose of showing that Jesus actually had divine authority, as had previously been suggested (7:29). This is followed by a teaching section (9:37–11:1), some of which seems to refer to the activities of the disciples following the death of Jesus (10:21-38) when they had to face persecution.

127 Did they not face persecution during Jesus' lifetime?

It is highly significant that though Jesus' preaching stirred up the Jews on numerous occasions, neither he nor his disciples suffered any physical harm previous to the crucifixion. The references to suffering and persecutions in Matthew reflect a condition with which the Christians of A.D. 80 (or 90) were well familiar. All this seems to indicate that at least some of these sayings were the product of post-resurrection days when the Christians believed the risen Lord walked and talked with them and gave them personal messages.

128 What is the basic message of the third section?

Again we find the familiar pattern—a series of incidents

(chaps. 11-12) followed by a sermon (13:1-52), which deals with the subject of the Kingdom of Heaven. Some of Jesus' most striking parables appear in this section. It seems to teach that the Kingdom is a mystery given to only a select inner circle of believers (13:13, 16, 17), but such is the divine power of the Kingdom that it needs no more than a planting to insure its ultimate possession of the field of the world (13:24-30, 37-43).

129 What is the basic message of the fourth section?

Once more the stereotyped form—narrative (14:1–17:27) and discourse (18:1-35). In the narrative section we come upon the bold declaration of Jesus' divine role in the story of the transfiguration (17:1-8), which follows Peter's confession of his Lord's messiahship (16:13-18). The story is fast approaching a climax.

The discourse section follows immediately and follows very naturally, being a series of instructions for the Christians (18:1-35). The student will be interested in comparing Matthew 16:19 with Matthew 18:18, and discovering that the powers conferred upon Peter in the first passage are conferred upon all the disciples in the second. (See also John 20:22-23).

130 What is the basic message of the fifth section?

The narrative portion of this section is a report of the journey to Jerusalem and the events which transpired in the capital (chaps. 19-23). In this case more teaching material than usual is included with the narrative. The general pattern follows closely the lines laid down in Mark's Gospel, and suggests something very interesting concerning the entire report contained in the Gospels. The discourse material is an attempt to turn the eyes of the Church toward the future, and at one point Matthew makes a definite attempt to awaken new interest and faith in the promise of the Master's return for a second ministry among men.

131 What is that interesting suggestion concerning the Gospel report?

We have already learned that the story of the resurrection of Jesus was the arresting message of the Christians. They went about everywhere proclaiming it. Their whole message revolved about it. A comparison of the story as it appears in the four Gospels reveals a marked similarity in the basic facts but a wide difference in detail. There are, for instance, four versions of the inscription that appeared on the cross above Jesus' head (Matthew 27:37; Mark 15:26; Luke 23:38; John 19:19). The accounts of the resurrection appearances differ so widely at points that it is impossible to reconcile them. Yet the basic fact of the empty tomb and the risen Lord is attested by all.

132 What do we conclude from all this?

It means that the story of the resurrection was told by the early Church with great detail, and that the writers of the four Gospels were influenced in their reports by variant versions. But it does not disturb the basic idea that Matthew thought of Jesus as being the Messiah and the world's teacher. This means that the Master who taught the way of life and the principles of the Kingdom was a man who spoke with divine authority back of his words. They were not merely the lovely words of a carpenter from Nazareth, but the revealed will of the Eternal God. To ignore them would be to imperil our very lives and our eternal salvation.

133 Did the Hebrew nation perish because it rejected Jesus?

The author of Matthew evidently believed this was true, and the words of the mob which he quotes—"His blood be on us and on our children" (27:25)—must have been a terrible reminder to a generation which had witnessed the carnage and terror attending the destruction of Jerusalem.

134 How does Matthew differ from Mark?

The difference between the two Gospels appears at a variety of points: (1) Mark portrays Jesus predominantly as a man of action, while Matthew represents him as a teacher. (2) Mark writes as though the question of Jesus' messiahship is to be kept in the background, while Matthew makes bold claims in Jesus' behalf in the matter. (3) Mark is content to tell the story of Jesus' activity, while Matthew undertakes to interpret it. (4) Mark seems to have been well acquainted with Old Testament prophecy, but it is Matthew who makes a deliberate attempt to prove that Jesus fulfilled the predictions. (5) Mark has little to say about the ancient Law, even going so far as to set it aside in some important matters (Mark 7:1-7); Matthew undertakes to show the contrast between the teachings of Jesus and the ancient Law on particular points, while insisting that Jesus fulfilled the Law.

135 What was the purpose of Matthew's Gospel?

There are those who think that Matthew wrote his Gospel for the purpose of setting forth the position of the Jewish wing of the Church, and there is some reason for thinking so. He declared the Law was to be observed (5:17, 18) and insisted that the teachings of the Pharisees were to be kept (23:3). He even seemed to limit Jesus' ministry to "the lost sheep of the house of Israel" (15:24). Moreover, Papias said that Matthew wrote in the Aramaic language—which may or may not have had significance.

On the other hand, there is a universal element in the Gospel which appears in numerous connections. People from everywhere are to be gathered into the Kingdom (8:11, 12); the disciples are to love all men (5:43-48); the Gentile Church is to take the place of the nation that has rejected Jesus (12:21; 21:33-43); the Gospel is to be preached to all nations (24:14).

All this might suggest that there were different groups inside the Christian Church which held varying opinions, and that Matthew was attempting to make room for all of them in the Christian movement. Or it might suggest that Matthew had not yet thought his way through on all the problems imposed upon the Church by the remarkable life and ministry of Jesus. At any rate, it is certain that Matthew is not a partisan and that he does not plead a particular viewpoint. Jesus was, to him, the long-looked-for Messiah of the Jews, and also the herald of the universal Kingdom of God, which he calls the Kingdom of Heaven.

136 How did Matthew compose his Gospel?

From our study of the Synoptics we learned that Matthew leaned heavily upon Mark's Gospel for his basic factual material concerning Jesus' activities. If we subtract the seven thousand words of Mark from the eight thousand words of Matthew's narrative material, we have very little original matter left. Some of Mark's reports are omitted by Matthew and slight changes are made here and there in specific statements, but for the most part it can be said that Matthew follows Mark.

Then there is in addition the discourse material of Matthew, shared in large part with Luke, which is believed to have come from some document or documents available to both writers. That the two Gospels correspond so closely in this discourse material seems ample proof that some such writing was in existence before A.D. 100, and that it later disappeared because it had been absorbed by the two.

That there may have been compilations and collections of stories, parables, testimonies of "fulfillments of prophecy," and teachings is entirely possible. Then in addition there is the independent material in both Matthew and Luke which is found nowhere else, which suggests that each had some private sources of information.

137 How extensive is Matthew's independent material?

It amounts to about four hundred verses out of the total, most of which consists of discoursive material. The principal narratives peculiar to Matthew consist of the Nativity stories (1:18-25; 2:1-18; 2:19-23), a portion of the story of Peter walking on the waves (14:28-33), the account of the coin found in the fish's mouth (17:24-27), portions of the story of the triumphal entry (21:10-11; 21:15-16), and certain details out of the Passion narrative (26:25; 26:52; 27:3 10; 27:19, 24-25, 51-53, 62-66; 28:2-4, 9-10, 11-15, 16-20).

By far the most of Matthew's material which is to be found nowhere else in the New Testament consists of sayings, teachings, parables, etc. For the best results it is recommended that the student study this subject with a good text showing the "harmony" of the Gospels in detail.

138 What special service does Matthew's Gospel render?

We have already learned that the writer was greatly interested in proving that Jesus was the Messiah of the Jews who had been foretold by the prophets. In doing so he was under the necessity of meeting certain objections raised by the Jews, and in this we probably get a reflection of the mind of the church of Jerusalem, and perhaps also that of Antioch.

139 What were those objections?

There was a rumor current among the Jews to the effect that Jesus' disciples had stolen his body and then proclaimed the resurrection. This Matthew refutes (28:15).

He knew that Jesus was widely accepted as a Nazarene (John 1:46; 7:41; 7:52) and for that reason makes it clear that actually he had been born at Bethlehem (Matthew 2:5), as Micah had prophesied (Micah 5:2), and that he had gone to live at Nazareth in order to fulfill another prophecy (2:23).

His ministry in Galilee had been foretold by Isaiah (4:13-14), therefore his messianic claims were to be accepted.

There was another rumor current in Palestine to the effect that Jesus had gone to Egypt to study magic, and this Matthew answers with the declaration that he had never been in Egypt except when he had gone there as a babe in arms according to another prophecy (Hosea 11:1).

140 How was the Gospel of Matthew received?

It seems to have taken first place in the affection of the Church almost from the start, perhaps because the name of Matthew was attached to it. At any rate, forty years afterward we find quotations from it in the writings of the Church Fathers. Still twenty years later, when the Ephesian church was gathering the Christian writings together, the book of Matthew was put at the head of the list of four Gospels, and there it has stood ever since. All this would indicate that it became immensely popular and must have exercised a powerful influence upon the infant Church.

141 What is the next Gospel to be studied?

The third and last of the Synoptics—the Gospel of Luke.

142 When was Luke written?

Any adequate answer to this question will depend upon a study of the book of Acts alongside the Gospel of Luke, but for the moment we can fix the date as about A.D. 90, though this is not proved and there remains some debate on the subject among scholars. Many believe, however, that it could not have been written far from that time, for Matthew and Luke seem to be independent of one another. Neither author seems to have copied from the other. Both seem to have consulted many of the same sources, and about the same religious situation is reflected in both Gospels. Therefore A.D. 90 is about as satisfactory a date as we can settle upon.

143 What does the book of Acts have to do with Luke?

Luke and Acts should be studied together for the reason that they were both written by the same author and are, actually, two volumes of the same work. There are those who believe the author may have intended originally to write three books, the third to tell the story of Paul's imprisonment and the subsequent development of the Christian Church. While there seems to be some evidence to support this theory, it can be no more than a theory and need not engage our attention beyond the mere mention. There is, however, one fact which should be considered.

144 What is that fact which should be considered?

The book of Acts closes with Paul in prison, his trial not yet having occurred. So far as the New Testament history is able to tell us, we know nothing of the final fate of the great Apostle. In view of the large place he occupies in the story which Acts tells, it is very strange that no report of the final outcome has been preserved. This would seem to indicate that a third book may have been planned.

In reading the Gospel of Luke and the book of the Acts we should keep in mind the fact that both were written approximately twenty-five years after the death of Paul and perhaps as much as sixty years following the death of Jesus. The story in the two books is told so skillfully and vividly that the reader is apt to get the impression that he is reading a contemporaneous account written by an eyewitness of all the events recorded. It is very important to an understanding of the books, then, that this late date be kept in mind at all times.

145 Who wrote the books of Luke and Acts?

The first thing for the student to note in seeking an answer to this question is that both books are anonymous. Neither makes any announcement of the name of the author, as do Revelation and the second and third epistles of John. Whatever we may decide in the matter must be dug out of the evidence in the books themselves, together with any outside references that may be available.

146 Where can we begin to look for evidence?

The opening verses of Luke throw light on our problem, and the first verse of Acts links the two books in a common authorship. Luke 1:1-4, however, is one of the most revealing passages in all the New Testament, for it throws much light on many literary problems in the Gospels.

147 What is the significance of the first verse of Luke?

It tells at least five vitally important facts: (1) The Gospels may not have been written by eyewitnesses, but certainly their authors could vouch for the reliability of the secondhand material with which they worked. (2) There were in existence other accounts written and oral, but none of them were orderly and satisfactorily complete. (3) The author of Luke has gone to great pains to verify his evidence, and has consulted earlier documents, including such information as he considered authentic. (4) He seems to have been in touch with living witnesses who could give him exact information. (5) He has written his account for a Greek Christian, the name "Theophilus" being Greek.

148 What does this passage prove?

It proves that the statements made concerning the existence of earlier documents used by Matthew, and perhaps by Mark, are essentially correct, and that our Gospels are the product of the labors of numerous writers and compilers. This means that the four Gospels are, in large part, the product of the Christian Church and not merely the work of four individual writers.

We have in the four Gospels documents which were subjected to the scrutiny of the entire Christian Church, and which were the accumulated result of the work of a considerable number of writers and compilers. They had to stand up in comparison with the oral tradition which had come down to the second generation of Christians. From all this it is easy to see that the opening verses of Luke's Gospel are highly important because of the light they throw upon the way the New Testament record of the life of Jesus was finally made up.

149 Who may the author of Luke's Gospel have been?

The name of Luke has been attached to the Gospel from a very early date. In fact, no other name has ever been given to it so far as we know, but we also know that this name was given to the book many years after it was originally written. At least, we have not been able to trace it back farther than the second century.

There is but one man named Luke who is mentioned in the early Christian records. He was a companion of Paul (Colossians 4:25; Philemon 24; II Timothy 4:11) of whom we know very little aside from the fact that he was a physician. He may have been converted under Paul's ministry at Troas, and may have been a member of the Christian congregation at that place (Acts 16:7-12). But at least he became a member of the Apostle's party in that city, whence they traveled to Philippi about A.D. 50.

150 What was Luke's mission with Paul's party?

There has been considerable speculation concerning this matter, and we can do no more than hazard a guess on the basis of the best information available. We know that Luke was a physician, and we also know that Paul suffered from some physical disability which he called a "thorn in the flesh" (II Corinthians 12:7). From these two facts it seems reasonable to assume that Luke accompanied the Apostle for professional reasons, though he may have been actuated primarily by powerful religious motives.

151 Do we know anything about his activities?

We know that after the Apostle's dream about the Macedonian man (Acts 16:9) who called for help, he left Troas with Paul (Acts 16:10-12) and went with him over into Europe. Having arrived in Philippi, he shared the ministry there, but when Paul and Silas went on to Thessalonica (Acts 17:1) Luke was left behind. He did not see Paul again for perhaps as much as five years, evidently remaining in Philippi (Acts 20:3-6) and probably becoming one of the pillars of the church there. When

Paul and Luke finally met again, they became inseparable companions, and Luke remained with the Apostle as long as we know anything about the movements of the two, and probably until Paul's death. Concerning the Macedonian vision, however, there is an extremely interesting theory.

152 What is the theory of the Macedonian vision?

In Acts 16:9 a "man of Macedonia" is mentioned as having appeared to Paul in a dream. No name is mentioned, but the peculiar Greek expression used in telling the story implies that the author could have named the individual if he had so desired, and some very excellent scholars have suggested that Luke was himself the man and that he was a native of Philippi.

Several facts support this theory. First, the name "Luke" is an abbreviation of a longer Greek name—*Lucanos*—somewhat as "Tim" is a nickname frequently used instead of "Timothy." This would identify the physician as a Gentile. That the author of Acts does not name the Macedonian can be explained on the basis of Luke's modesty—he might not have desired to mention himself. When they have arrived in Philippi, he says, "Where we supposed there was a place of prayer" (Acts 16:13), intimating that he was a resident of Philippi who knew that the little colony of Jews had some meeting place for prayer but was not exactly informed as to its precise whereabouts. In describing Philippi (Acts 16:12) the author refers to it as a Roman colony and *the first of the district*, but there were other cities mentioned in Acts which were also Roman colonies—Corinth, Lystra, Ptolemais, Pisidian Antioch, etc.—and that fact is not mentioned. This would suggest that Luke took some pride in his home city and gave it special mention. This assumption is strengthened by the fact that he calls it the first of the district, a designation which would certainly have been disputed by Thessalonica or Amphipolis. It is in connection with the Philippian ministry that we are provided with one of our most valuable bits of information concerning the authorship of Acts and Luke's Gospel—namely the use of the word "we."

153 What is important about the word "we"?

The story of the book of Acts runs along very smoothly as a bit of historical writing produced by one who was no party to the events described until we come to Acts 16:10, when suddenly the word "we" appears, as though the author has now become a part of the story. The use of "we" continues on to the end of the chapter, as though it is a personal report. With the beginning of chapter 17 Paul is mentioned as being on a missionary journey to Thessalonica, and again the story is told in third personal terms until we come to 20:5, when the author includes himself again. Four such sections (Acts 16:10-17; 20:5-16; 21:1-18; 27:1–28:16) are known to Bible students as the "we sections" of Acts. They identify the author as a participant in the events described; for, when we compare these sections with what we know about Luke's movements, it becomes apparent that Luke refers to himself when he says "we." This goes far toward establishing Luke's authorship of Acts and, in turn, of the Gospel of Luke. From all the references to him in the New Testament (Acts 16:10; 20:3-5; 21:15; 27; Colossians 4:14; Philemon 24) it would appear that, though Luke may not have shared largely in the evangelistic work, he may have spent his time serving Paul and engaging in literary work.

154 What happened to Luke after Paul's death?

There is no authentic history upon which we can rely, though there is a tradition to the effect that he lived to the age of seventy-four, that he never married, and that he finally died in Constantinople. In the city of Padua, in Italy, there is a sarcophagus in the Church of Santa Giustina which was brought there from Constantinople and which is shown to visitors as being Luke's, but all this, of course, is subject to serious doubt.

155 Does all this prove that Luke wrote the Gospel?

It does not, but it lends great credibility to that belief. Since there is no other theory that needs to be considered seriously, however, we shall proceed with our study on the assumption that it is true that Luke, Paul's physician, is the author of the Gospel which bears his name, and also of the Acts of the Apostles. Certainly such an assumption explains many things about the books.

156 Was Luke prepared to write?

Though we have no knowledge whatever of Luke's scholastic

training, we do know that he was a learned man; for (1) he was a physician, and this called for some type of formal training, and (2) his writing shows the marks of much literary ability, historical sense, and general learning. In weighing the importance of Luke's writings, however, we must get a clear picture of the circumstances under which he wrote.

157 What was peculiar about those circumstances?

Luke's meeting with Paul occurred only a short time before the Apostle's journey into Macedonia, which must be dated about twenty years after the death of Jesus. His writing was done a generation later, so that it represents the Christian Church as of at least the second generation after Jesus' death. The Christians for whom Luke wrote were face to face with an entirely different set of problems from those which the first generation had had to meet. If we will keep seven facts in mind, they will assist us greatly in understanding Luke's writings.

158 What were the seven problems the Christians faced?

1. The Christian movement was under dire threat from the empire.
2. Heresies were multiplying inside the Christian movement.
3. The Christian message had to be adapted to the Greek mind.
4. The Christian movement had enlisted large numbers of the poor.
5. There was confusion concerning details in the life and teachings of Jesus.
6. Several written records concerning Jesus were in circulation among the Christians.
7. Christianity had to meet bitter opposition from the Jews.

159 What was the threat of the empire?

In other studies mention has been made of the persecutions which were falling upon the Church. It is very evident that Luke's Gospel was a serious effort to present the entire Christian movement in its most favorable light. He sought to show that opposition had originated, not in any deliberate offense on the part of the Christians, but in the bitter enmity of the Jews. He portrays Jesus as a gentle teacher with a profound interest in the poor, and in no sense a political agitator or disturber. His death was brought about by bigoted Jews in spite of Roman officials who actually tried to befriend him. With great care he points out the fact that on at least four occasions (23:4; 23:11; 23:14; 23:20) he was acquitted by Roman officers. All this, and more, in the Gospel of Luke seems to be a frank appeal for fair treatment at the hands of the Romans, who have no cause for complaint against the Christian movement.

160 What about the heresies?

These were disruptive movements originating inside the Christian fellowship itself. We have learned from various other studies how serious the situation became toward the close of the second century. The Gospel of Luke aims to set the whole matter right by presenting a straightforward account of Christianity which would leave no room for doubt. Luke states very frankly (1:1-3) in his introduction that it is his purpose to provide the world with an account of the movement which will clear up misunderstandings. He addresses his work to "most excellent Theophilus," but it is clearly intended as a literary work for all people everywhere.

161 Who was Theophilus?

Aside from the mention of his name in the Gospel of Luke (1:3) and in the Acts of the Apostles (1:1), there is no record of any such individual in the New Testament. The name means in Greek "friend of God," and some have thought it might have been a general title, like "Mr. Greatheart," or "Beloved Colleague." The title "most excellent" suggests, however, that the man may have been a Greek nobleman, or, as some think, a Roman official. If this were true it would lend additional import to Luke's efforts to present the Christian movement in its most favorable light. In the absence of any positive identification, however, we must be content to believe that Theophilus was no more than a worthy Greek who was profoundly interested in Christianity (1:4) and who sought authentic reports and interpretations thereof. These Luke undertook to supply, and in making them available to Theophilus and his friends he made them available to men of all time since. There are those who make the interesting suggestion that Theophilus was a man of wealth whose generosity provided the means which supported Luke while he gathered his materials and committed them to writing.

162 **What about the adaptation of the Christian message to Greeks?**

By A.D. 90 the Christian movement was almost entirely divorced from its Jewish origins. The Jerusalem church had either passed out of existence or ceased to be an influence in the movement. Following the death of Paul the leadership of the movement passed over almost entirely into the hands of Greeks. Paul's letters to the churches had been written for Gentiles and in the Greek language, but they had been written by a Jew. It was inevitable that some Greek should write for Greek Christians, putting the great Christian convictions into their language as a Greek would express them. This was exactly what Luke did.

163 **Were the Christians all poor people?**

The student will remember the Paul entered the city of Thessalonica as an unemployed sailmaker, and that his first hearers were workingmen whom he met in the shops and market places. The same was true in Corinth and probably in other great cities. Certainly we know that there were occasional individuals of social importance who came into the Church, but for the most part the early Christians were recruited from among the poor, many of them probably being slaves. (See I Corinthians 1:26-29).

164 **Did this make any difference in Luke's Gospel?**

It is one of the outstanding characteristics of Luke's Gospel that he gives much attention to the poor. He pictures the door of the Bethlehem inn closed on Jesus' mother (2:7) and quotes her as singing a song that is almost boastful as she exults over the rich and the mighty (1:52-53). In Jesus' first sermon in Nazareth he talks about "good news to the poor" (4:18). In one of his beatitudes he speaks of the poor who are blessed and adds "woe to you that are rich!" (6:24) whereas Matthew speaks only of those who are "poor in spirit" (Matthew 5:3). Luke counsels the Christians to entertain the poor instead of the rich (14:13), and in his story of the great supper he speaks of the poor and the maimed (14:21). Only in his Gospel do we find the story of the rich man and Lazarus, and the parable of the rich fool who built bigger barns. There are those who find in this a hint as to Luke's personal prejudices.

165 How could Luke have been prejudiced?

It was a rather common thing for rich Greeks to educate some bright and promising slave boy for the practice of medicine or some other art or science. Thereafter such a slave would become a part of the family establishment. Some have suggested that Theophilus was such a rich man and that Luke may have been his slave, becoming Paul's companion and physician as a result of the nobleman's generosity. If this is true (and it is no more than a conjecture), Luke's experience as a slave would undoubtedly have made him considerate of the poor and perhaps even prejudiced in their favor.

166 Why should the Christians be confused about Jesus?

We must continue to remember that the Christians for whom Luke wrote were at least one generation removed from Jesus. Communication between Christian congregations was haphazard at best, with the result that a doctrine emphasized in one community might be neglected in another, and that stories and teachings of Jesus which received much attention inside one group might receive less attention inside another. It would be perfectly natural for instance, that Paul's personal beliefs would have great influence in one church with which he had intimate connections, and that Apollos' teachings would weigh heavily in another congregation which had never known Paul. Then too, the written documents probably did not circulate equally or evenly in all the churches. That is certainly true in our times. One congregation of Christians will lay great emphasis on Daniel and Revelation (perhaps under the leadership of their minister), and another will make much of the Fourth Gospel, with two entirely different teachings resulting. Luke seems to have written for the purpose of producing an account of

Christian faith and history which could be accepted everywhere.

167 For what purpose was Luke's Gospel written?

Within half a century after the death of Jesus, Christianity had become a Greek enterprise, and its success was so marked that individuals here and there began to dream that it might become a world religion. If this should occur, some record must be made of its origins, message, and general history before it was too late. Luke distinctly states that he set out to do that very thing, "to write an orderly account" (1:3).

168 Why were the Jews so opposed to Christianity?

This matter has already been dealt with in our study of the Fourth Gospel, Revelation, and Matthew. It is sufficient here to remind ourselves that the Jews looked upon Christians as apostates, and that their jealousy was heightened by the fact that Christianity attracted many Greeks who had gone over to Judaism and who then turned to Christianity as a still more adequate faith.

169 What about those written records of the movement?

Just how many there were we cannot be sure, though we know there were several. (1) There was Mark's Gospel, of course, which seems to have circulated rather widely among Christians. We have already learned that Matthew used it in a large way. (2) Then there seems to have been the document which we have called "Q." (3) There may have been tracts and smaller books such as the record of the controversies, the "wonder book" relative to the resurrection, etc. (4) We know that Matthew had independent sources of information, some of which may have been written records, and so did Luke. All these needed to be correlated and organized into one orderly account.

170 How did Luke use Mark's Gospel?

If the student will read Luke alongside Mark, he will make the simple discovery that at least five rather extended sections are based on similar passages taken from Mark:

The Gospel of Mark includes a total of 666 verses, of which Luke has borrowed more than half. Of the 1,151 verses of Luke's Gospel, at least thirty per cent have been taken from Mark. It is especially interesting to note that when Luke does borrow from Mark he preserves his order and sequence with great care. He adds no notations of time or place where Mark does not supply them. All this is important for two reasons.

171 **What is the first reason why this is important?**

The fact that both Matthew and Luke so generously used Mark indicates that the first-century Christian Church recognized this Gospel as the authoritative statement of the facts. If the tradition is correct that Mark drew a considerable part of his information from Peter, then that may explain much concerning his Gospel. But even if it be not true, the very fact that the Gospel was accepted as being trustworthy puts the authority of the first-century Christian Church behind it. We can accept it with confidence because the Christians of A.D. 80-90 accepted it.

172 **What is the second reason for the importance of the use of Mark?**

With clear evidence before us that Luke used Mark without altering his style, his sequence, or his statements of fact, we have good reason to believe that Luke was equally honest with other documents he may have used, even though his arrangement of the material differs from Matthew's.

173 **What is the difference between the two?**

Matthew had a system by which he presented a narrative followed by discoursive material. The Sermon on the Mount is an excellent illustration. In Matthew it is found in one compact section, unassociated with narrative material. In Luke, on the other hand, it is found scattered throughout the Gospel in fragmentary form. Matthew evidently collected and arranged this material, while Luke seems to have presented it piece by piece, more nearly as it may have appeared in the original form. Perhaps we have here a hint as to the purpose back of Q.

174 What could that purpose have been?

The Q document evidently contained an assortment of sayings of Jesus—words, teachings, admonitions, advices, warnings. It seems to have contained no reports of miracles, and only a few parables. As soon as Christianity began to spread as a result of the preaching of Jesus' resurrection, the converts began to feel the need of specific instructions concerning the Christian way of life. A long list of problems arose, many of them involving moral decisions both delicate and difficult. What had Jesus said about prayer, riches, faith, social relations, etc.? Someone (or perhaps several people) gathered together fragments and notes from Jesus' preaching which were intended to serve as something like a guide for Christian life and conduct, and this in time became the Q document.

175 How much independent material did Luke use?

Almost half of the Gospel of Luke is made up of material not to be found anywhere else in the New Testament. Some of it may have come from Q, but of that we have no proof. It is material of the same sort that we would expect to have found in Q, but it may have come from another source. All we know is that Luke alone uses it.

Again we suggest that the student procure a harmony of the Gospels which shows their correspondences in parallel columns. Let him note the amount of material, and its nature, contained exclusively in Luke. This is a study well worth the cost of such a "harmony" as well as the time necessary to make the study.

As a special characteristic of the third Gospel it is interesting to note that Luke has preserved at least six incidents in connection with which Jesus prayed (3:21; 5:16; 6:12; 9:29; 23:34; 23:46). In something of the manner of the Fourth Gospel, Luke records the effect of Jesus' words or acts upon those who witnessed them (4:15; 9:43; 18:43). And, in contrast with Matthew, he preserves the connection in which the various sayings were first uttered. In justification of his claim that he has undertaken to present the record accurately, fully, in order, and after careful research, it is worthy of note that Luke takes great pains to give dates, times, and places. Except for his Gospel we should have very few genuinely historical dates preserved for us.

176 Where did Luke get his independent material?

It must have come to him from three sources: (1) Many scholars believe he had access to some document similar to Q. He may, indeed, have used several such. (2) He had numerous contacts with individuals who are known to have been in a position to supply him with exact information. (3) He had at least one experience which must have opened up for him several valuable sources of information.

177 What about the unknown documents?

Scholars believe that there may have been at least one such, and to it they have given the name "L." It is possible, of course, that Luke found more material in Q suited to his purpose than Matthew did, and that the so-called independent material of Luke is composed in part of additional quotations from Q. This, however, cannot be more than a conjecture. The resurrection story seems to have assumed some fixed form throughout the Church, and there may have been a document in circulation which told this story in an abbreviated form. Then there are those who believe that the Nativity stories in Luke rest back on an Aramaic document which was associated in some way with Mary the mother of Jesus. All these can be no more than surmises even though they may be very probable surmises.

178 What about the individuals who had information?

There was, first of all, the Apostle Paul. It is known that Luke traveled with him for a considerable time, and it is also known that Paul could quote from sayings of Jesus which are not to be found in any of our Gospels (Acts 20:35). Much original material must have been in Paul's possession, even though he made small use of any historical data relative to Jesus in any of his letters to the churches. What developed in private conversations between Paul and Luke cannot even be guessed.

Then there was the Jewish Christian Silas, who was another of Paul's traveling companions for at least a part of the time, and from whom Luke must have learned a great many interesting things concerning the early experiences of the Christian Church at Jerusalem. (Acts 16:10 ff.; see also 15:22, 27, 32, 40.) As a traveling companion of Paul during those last tragic days, Luke must have come in contact with many prominent Christians from whom much exact information could have been obtained. In Jerusalem he was present with Paul when the Apostle conferred with James the Lord's brother and the leaders of the Jerusalem church (Acts 21:17-18). At Caesarea Philippi he was housed with the family of Philip the evangelist and there met the daughters of the house, who were women of character and importance in their own right. (Acts 21:8-9). There also he met a prophet from Jerusalem known as Agabus (Acts 11:27-28). On another occasion he seems to have been a member of a group of disciples of whom Mark was another (Colossians 4:10; Philemon 24). All these persons should have contributed much to Luke's general fund of information concerning Jesus and the early days of the Christian movement.

179 What about the unusual experience Luke had?

Following his arrest in Jerusalem, Paul was incarcerated in the prison at Caesarea Philippi for a period of two years (Acts 23:23; 24:27) awaiting trial. During that time Luke was near at hand and must have had considerable opportunity to gather much exact information concerning the various matters of historical interest. Mary, the mother of Jesus, could still have been living, and Luke could have made a visit to Nazareth to interview her if he had desired to do so. There would most surely have been others living (A.D. 60) who could have furnished Luke with firsthand information, and many scholars believe he occupied his time during those two years gathering data and verifying facts which he incorporated into his Gospel many years later.

180 Where was the Gospel of Luke written?

There is an ancient version of the book of Acts which contains a very interesting reading. "In those days prophets came down from Jerusalem to Antioch [in Syria]," it says. "And there was great exultation: and when we had assembled, one of them, by name Agabus, spoke, etc." (Acts 11:27-28.) This would be the earliest "we passage" in the entire book of Acts if this version could be proved correct, and it would put Luke back to about A.D. 40 in Antioch. Now it happens that Antioch is mentioned thirteen times, and in at least two instances (Acts 11:19-27; 13:1 ff.) there seems to be evident considerable firsthand knowledge of the city. The church at Antioch was a very important congregation and a center of Christian influence throughout the East. Some of the Church Fathers hint that Luke was a man of Antioch, and others suggest other origins for him. Upon the basis of this uncertain evidence, it has been suggested that Luke's Gospel may have been written in Antioch, although this cannot be exactly determined. It is enough to say that he was a Gentile and wrote for the Gentiles.

181 How does Luke's Gospel differ from Matthew's?

In at least three aspects: (1) literary style, (2) content, and (3) objective.

182 How do their literary styles differ?

Luke's Gospel bears evidence of having been written by a man of unusual literary ability who was familiar with the written styles of classical Greek. In some passages—his dignified introduction, for example—he followed the stately style of the professional writers of the day. In many of his chapters, on the other hand, we find him using the colloquial style of the common people. Yet when all its common usages are conceded, it still remains true that his work is of much better literary quality than either Matthew or Mark. This is due, no doubt, to the fact that it was written by one who spoke in his native tongue without the necessity of translating ideas or words. Renan, the great French skeptic, called the Gospel of Luke "the most beautiful book ever written."

183 How does it differ in content from Matthew?

In the first place, the Nativity stories with which it opens are entirely different from those told by Matthew. Luke tells the story of the shepherds, for instance, and Matthew the story of the wise men. Then, in addition and in much the same strain, Luke includes a story concerning the birth of John the Baptist which is to be found nowhere else in the New Testament. Mary plays a role in Luke's narrative which is not even hinted at in

Matthew's story. Luke's genealogy differs sharply from that of Matthew, a remarkable story of Jesus' visit to the temple is told in a few brief verses, and the Holy Spirit is represented as playing a role quite different from that described in any of the other three Gospels.

184 What about Luke's Nativity story?

It will be remembered that in Matthew's report of the birth of Jesus the Virgin Mother was kept in the background, while the scene was filled with wise men, angels, kings, and visions. If we had no other Gospel than Matthew's upon which to rely for information, we should not have one recorded word of Mary's, nor should we know more than a few of the simplest facts about her.

In Luke's Gospel the mother of Jesus occupies the stage from beginning to end. Her hymns are recorded in the first two chapters and constitute what must have been the beginning of Christian hymnody. The visit between Mary and Elizabeth, before the birth of either son, is an obvious attempt to link the careers of the two famous preachers. The fullness of these stories has encouraged some scholars to believe strongly that Luke had had conversations with the Virgin Mother. Since he seems to have been unusually well informed concerning Herod, it is possible that one of the Christians whose acquaintance he made while in Caesarea was Joanna, the wife of Chuza, Herod's steward (Luke 8:3).

185 Is there any significance in the story of John's unusual birth?

We know that John's movement continued for many years after the prophet's death, and that the author of the Fourth Gospel found it necessary to take it into account (John 1:6 ff.). It is entirely possible that the story of the Baptist's miraculous birth which appears in Luke's Gospel may be one that was preserved by the Johnites and taken over by Luke.

186 What about Luke's genealogy?

It will be recalled that Matthew's Gospel carries Jesus' ancestry back to Abraham (Matthew 1:1-2), but Luke carries it back to Adam (Luke 3:23-38). This seems to be an effort on the part of a Gentile writer to include all men in the audience to whom the good news of redemption is to be preached. Jesus is no longer merely the Messiah of the Jewish nation, but the Saviour of all men. This is called the "universalism" of Luke's Gospel—the evangelist's interest in the good news for all humanity. This appears in at least two other Lucan passages.

187 How does Luke reveal his universalism?

As a Gentile Christian, Luke would be very naturally interested in the mission to the non-Jewish population of the world. He therefore indicates in both Luke and Acts that the gospel, first offered to the Jews, was rejected by them, and was then preached to the Gentiles. In the Gospel, for instance, he tells the story of Jesus' rejection at the hands of his fellow townsmen of Nazareth (4:16-22), and a similar situation is described in Acts (4:1-21) in which the nation repudiated its own Messiah, whereupon the Gospel is carried out to the Gentile world.

188 What about the Holy Spirit in the Gospel of Luke?

Luke seems to have had a special interest in the work and function of the Holy Spirit. He represents the Spirit as being active in the advent of Jesus to the earth. Prompted by the Holy Spirit, Mary sings. Every now and again the term appears in the narrative as though referring to a personal agent. The gift of the Spirit of God is, to Luke, the supreme contribution of God to man. But this must not blind us to the fact that Luke also had a very profound social concern.

189 How was Luke concerned socially?

He seems to have had what was almost a prejudice against wealth. The man who lays up treasure on earth is little more than a fool. Luke knows of but one good use to which money can be put, and that is that it be given away. It is not that Luke had any idea of upsetting the social order, for he did not. He had no social program; he had only a great desire to relieve poverty.

190 How was the Gospel of Luke received?

Renan is not the only one who was paid tribute to the literary quality of Luke. Other masters of literary expression have given the little book equally high praise. Certainly some of our most beautiful Christian concepts, notably in connection with Christmas and Easter, are derived from the Gospel of Luke. To this day it stands supreme in the field of religion as a beautiful expression of divine truth. As a piece of artistry there is nothing in the New Testament to compare with it. As a piece of religious literature it represents Christian faith at its best. It is just here, perhaps, that one of its most peculiar characteristics appears.

191 What is that peculiarity?

In spite of the fact that Luke was the companion of Paul, the great Christian theologian, his own work is in no sense theological. Rather, it is a tender, human, gentle, and profoundly devotional piece of writing. There have been those who have tried to find evidence of Luke and physician in the familiarity with which medical terms, instruments, and facts are mentioned. Others have tried to make of him a social reformer. But he fits into but one niche—that of a devout historian who has tried to give an accurate, orderly, truthful account of the way a great hope dawned upon the consciousness of men.

192 What was his great contribution?

Mark and Matthew were interested in portraying Jesus in such a way that men might be convinced that he was the Messiah of the Jews. Luke, on the other hand, is interested in showing what kind of man he was, in the hope that others may accept him as their redeemer and guide to God. Having set Jesus forth in such a character, he was next ready to trace the story of the rise and growth of the Christian movement.

193 How did he do that?

By publishing the Acts of the Apostles.

194 What is the Acts of the Apostles?

It is our only history of the Christian movement which tells what happened during the first century of the faith's existence. The title is misleading, because it is not, strictly speaking, a record of the activities of the eleven original disciples of Jesus but, rather, a history of the expanding church in which two characters—Peter and Paul—occupy the center of the stage for the most of the time.

195 How did the book get its name?

This we do not know, for it is not a part of the original writing of Luke. Apparently it is a title that became affixed by popular usage during the years following its first publication. Again we must be reminded that the ancient writers did not give titles to their books.

196 What happened to the original disciples?

Concerning their activities and later work we have little exact knowledge. Only two get any important mention in the Acts of the Apostles—Peter and John—and only one—Peter—really figures conspicuously as the tale unfolds. They seem to have made Jerusalem their headquarters, and may have conducted missionary activities in various parts of the world. The Roman Catholic church perpetuates numerous legends concerning them, claiming martyrdom for all but John. These legends, however, are of dubious historical worth for the most part and can for lack of space, be dismissed in such a study as this. In Acts others than the disciples, for the most part, take the lead. Stephen, a Hellenist, is the first martyr (Acts 6:1-5; 7:57-58); Philip the evangelist is the first to preach to the Gentiles (Samaritans—8:5), he being another Hellenist; Barnabas, one of Paul's companions, took charge of the first mission to the Greeks (11:22-23); James, the brother of Jesus and not one of the original disciples, rose to leadership in the Jerusalem church very soon after its organization (12:17; 15:13; 21:18). A more accurate title for the book would be "The Acts of Peter and Paul," for these two are the leading characters in the story as Luke tells it.

197 When was Acts written?

There is considerable disagreement on this subject, with excellent scholars taking widely divergent positions. There are those who would date the book as early as 56 or 57, and others who insist it could not possibly have been written before A.D. 90. Those who argue for the early date declare the book would not have closed without some word concerning Paul's fate if that fate had been known to the writer at the time of writing. Others argue that Luke was probably expecting to write a third volume dealing with the story of the trial, and thus complete the account. This hypothesis would assume that he was prevented from doing so, or that his third volume has been lost in some mysterious way. There are those who believe that Luke 21 contains a hint of the fall of Jerusalem, which occurred in A.D. 70; if that be true, then both Luke and Acts must have been written after that date. We can be sure that Acts was written later than Luke. About the best we can do is to leave the question open with the assumption that it was probably written sometime between the years 80 and 90.

198 Could Luke have written Acts in A.D. 90?

We know that he met Paul in Troas about A.D. 50. He seems to have been a young man at the time. If we assume that he was then no more than thirty years of age, he would have been only seventy by A.D. 90. To write such a book at such an age would have been entirely possible. In the meantime his long service in behalf of the Church, together with his exceptional opportunities for investigating and searching for facts, would have prepared him in an unusual way for the responsibility of authorship.

199 Upon what sources did he draw in writing Acts?

Just here we come upon one of the most interesting aspects of the entire book—and of the historical books of the New Testament, for that matter. We have already learned that the four Gospels were in no case written by eyewitnesses of the events described. They were based on documents and oral tradition that had come down from earlier days. In the case of Acts, however, we come upon an entirely different situation. The first fifteen chapters consist of material gleaned from a variety of sources, but beginning with the sixteenth chapter (16:10-17) we find a series of records which directly claim to be eyewitness reports (16:10-17; 20:5-15; 21:1-18; 27:1–28:16). These are the famous "we" sections already mentioned. There are those who believe they may have been taken from a travel diary kept by some member of Paul's party, but most scholars believe they identify Luke as the author. Some believe they may be notes from Luke's own diary kept while in company with Paul. In any case we get the impression that we are here for the first time dealing with a record written by one who was on the ground and saw what he is describing. This is something new in New Testament history.

In addition to the personal reports in the "we" sections, there seems to be some evidence that at least a portion of the other material was gleaned from written documents. Knowing how Luke worked with original documents in composing his Gospel, we should not be surprised if he used the same method in composing Acts. In addition to the foregoing, there seems to be at least some material which is the product of Luke's own creation.

200 What is Luke's own contribution to the book?

In several instances there are extended speeches reported in the book which, from the very nature of the case, could not have been prepared addresses committed to writing, and some of which Luke could not have heard with his own ears. Stephen's defense (7:1-53) must have been delivered extemporaneously, and could hardly have been taken down stenographically and preserved for us in its present form. Instead, the report we have in Acts must surely be a reconstruction which Luke worked out on the basis of such oral reports as he was able to gather together. A conspicuous illustration of this same situation is the case of Peter's speech at Pentecost, which seems to have been attended by so many wonderful circumstances. As this address appears in Acts, it must surely be a reconstruction and not a verbatim report. Then there is Paul's speech at Antioch in Pisidia (13:16-41), and his address on Mars' Hill (17:22-31). In these cases Luke must have heard Paul tell the story, together with at least a synopsis of the addresses delivered on those occasions, and from these Luke probably compiled his account.

201 For what purpose was Acts written?

The author states his purpose very plainly in the beginning of this book. He is undertaking to explain to Theophilus (and incidentally to the world) the circumstances under which the Christian faith rose to power and began its sweep across the earth. It by now appeared to be on its way to becoming a world religion, and some account of its origins was necessary if it was to appeal to cultured and learned people.

There are those who think the book may have been prepared

as a defense of the Christians in their conflict with the empire, and possibly as a special defense of Paul, who was on trial in Caesar's court. Some credence is lent to this belief by the fact that the attitude of the book toward the empire is extremely ingratiating.

202 What could be accomplished by that?

If the Roman empire could be persuaded that it had nothing to fear at the hands of the Christians, and that they were an altogether peaceful group with no evil designs upon the empire, it might make life much easier for Christians everywhere.

203 How does Luke proceed in that regard?

It will be remembered that in the Gospel, Luke reports four acquittals for Jesus at the hands of Roman officers, with the final blame for his crucifixion laid at the feet of the Jews. In the Acts of the Apostles we find numerous instances in which the writer seems to have gone out of his way to show that some local Roman who was close to the facts had shown marked consideration for the Christians, as a consequence of which the empire should be persuaded to show them leniency generally. Wherever they came into conflict with the Roman officers, they were acquitted or shown good will. Indeed, from chapter 16 onward we are treated to one instance after another in which Paul is shown courtesy at the hands of the government officials. The magistrates of Philippi free Paul even before he makes known the fact that he is a Roman citizen; the politarchs of Thessalonica refuse to listen to the accusations against him; a Corinthian judge dismisses the charges against him and shows his contempt for his accusers; the Asiarchs of Ephesus stand up for him, and the town clerk pronounces him innocent and peaceable. Claudius Lysias at Jerusalem treats him with marked respect; Felix and Festus, the procurators, refuse to hand him over to his enemies; and Agrippa II acquits him completely. There is no record of any formal charge having been made against him at Rome, and he is allowed generous liberty while awaiting trial.

204 What plan does Luke follow in Acts?

The book sets out to show the process by which the Christian Church developed out of a small band that declared its faith in the resurrection of Jesus, the Messiah, into a world-wide movement. There was first the local group of Christians in Jerusalem; then the movement began to spread among Hellenists; and finally it became divorced from the Jewish nation entirely.

In working out the story Luke divides his book into two great sections: (1) the history of the Christian Church through its early days under Jewish influence and its later ascendancy over it, and (2) its history as a great Gentile enterprise.

205 Is this division clearly marked?

As a matter of fact, the author seems to have divided his work into six parts, each of which closes with a formula which indicates that one more step has been taken in the process of telling the story:
1. The first days of the church at Jerusalem, 1:2–6:6
2. The flow of the faith out into Palestine, 6:8–9:30
3. From Palestine to Antioch in Syria, 9:32–12:23
4. From Syria to Asia Minor, 12:25–16:4
5. Paul at work in Europe, 16:6–19:19
6. Paul's last days, chapters 20–28

206 Can Luke be regarded as an accurate historian?

This question can be answered in the affirmative and, strangely enough, in the negative. This calls for some explanation.

207 How can it be answered in the affirmative?

The book is full of historical, geographical, and political references which indicate that Luke was familiar with his material and that he had gone to great pains to verify his statements. He knows, for instance, that Cyprus was governed by a proconsul and gives his correct name (13:7); Philippi was a Roman colony whose magistrates were called "praetors" and who were attended by "lictors" (16:20, 35); the magistrates of Thessalonica, on the other hand, were called "politarchs" (17:6); officers of the province of Asia were called "Asiarchs" (19:31). It would be possible to extend this list considerably, and all this would indicate that Luke was an accurate and careful historian.

208 How can it be answered negatively?

Strangely enough, the author of Acts never hints that he ever heard of Paul's writing a letter to anyone. If he ever knew of such epistles as that to the Romans, which must have been written while Luke was traveling with Paul, he never drops a hint to that effect. Then in addition he is either ignorant of, or unimpressed by, many of Paul's personal experiences. In II Corinthians 11:24-28 the Apostle mentions at least thirteen deadly dangers through which he has passed, only two of which Luke mentions. Then too, Paul tells of a mission to Illyricum (Romans 15:19) of which Luke seems to be uninformed, or at least of which he makes no mention. If he was trying to write a complete history, he failed—but perhaps he was trying to write something else.

209 What was he trying to do?

Both the Gospel and Acts are of such length that they would fill the average roll of papyrus. Evidently the author was under the necessity of compressing all his material within a limited space. We know he omitted some rather important sections of Mark in crowding his Gospel into the narrow limits available, and it is reasonable to assume that he resorted to the same device in the case of the Acts of the Apostles. He had to limit himself to certain incidents which would best show how the Christian movement spread. If we read his book with this in mind, we shall readily agree that the incidents he selected were all significant and carry his point very satisfactorily.

210 What is our judgment of Luke, then?

There seems to have been considerable confusion in and out of the Christian Church during the first century. No records were kept; the historian was at the mercy of hearsay; oral tradition played a conspicuous part; personal reminiscences, conflicting opinions, and fleeting rumors all entered into the picture. Luke undoubtedly took great pains to make sure of his facts, but even so errors crept in. There are three accounts of Paul's conversion, for instance (chaps. 9, 22, 26), which agree in the main facts but disagree in numerous details. In 9:7 Paul's companions hear a voice but see nothing; in 22:9 they hear nothing but see a light; in 26:13-14 they hear and see nothing,

othing but see a light; in 26:13-14 they hear and see nothing, it they fall to the ground speechless. It is possible to believe that Paul told the story with varying details under different circumstances, but even under the errors and discrepancies of these three reports we sense the feeling of great awe in the presence of a miracle that is taking place. A new faith is rapidly taking the world captive in the name of a Palestinian peasant who knows his way to the heart of God and is leading other men to that exquisite experience.

211 What are the characteristics of Luke's writing of Acts?

He takes great delight in reciting the miraculous. Angels, appearances, divine interventions, and supernatural occurrences are frequent. Certainly he believed that the new religion had come from God and that signs and wonders were to be expected.

In addition he assigns great importance to the joy that attends those who have had this experience with God. New converts are received into the Church with great joy; there is a spirit of gladness in the book in spite of the dangers that surge up through its pages from beginning to end.

212 What contribution has Luke made to the Christian faith?

In Luke and Acts this Gentile physician, who seems to withdraw modestly from his own pages, has made a contribution to the faith of Christians that cannot be estimated. The sheer beauty and candor of his writing is not to be excelled in all the New Testament. No small part of the Gospel story would have been lost to us except for his meticulous care in tracing down facts and events, and without his history of those first crucial years in the life of the Church we should be utterly without a record of any kind. Let every Christian, therefore, give profound and hearty thanks for the labors of this gentle man who loved his Lord, the poor, and the Church so faithfully and so unselfishly.